Is Your Museum

Grant-Ready?

ABOUT THE SERIES
The American Association for State and Local History Book Series publishes technical and professional information for those who practice and support history, and addresses issues critical to the field of state and local history. To submit a proposal or manuscript to the series, please request proposal guidelines from AASLH headquarters: AASLH Book Series, 1717 Church St., Nashville, Tennessee 37203. Telephone: (615) 320-3203. Fax: (615) 327-9013. Website: www.aaslh.org.

ABOUT THE ORGANIZATION
The American Association for State and Local History (AASLH) is a nonprofit educational organization dedicated to advancing knowledge, understanding, and appreciation of local history in the United States and Canada. In addition to sponsorship of this book series, the association publishes the periodical *History News*, a newsletter, technical leaflets and reports, and other materials; confers prizes and awards in recognition of outstanding achievement in the field; and supports a broad education program and other activities designed to help members work more effectively. To join the organization, contact: Membership Director, AASLH, 1717 Church St., Nashville, Tennessee 37203.

Is Your Museum Grant-Ready?

Assessing Your Organization's Potential for Funding

SARAH S. BROPHY

ALTAMIRA
PRESS

A Division of
ROWMAN AND LITTLEFIELD PUBLISHERS, INC.
Lanham   New York   Toronto   Oxford

AltaMira Press
A division of Rowman & Littlefield Publishers, Inc.
A wholly owned subsidary of The Rowman & Littlefield Publishing Group, Inc.
4501 Forbes Boulevard, Suite 200
Lanham, MD 20706
www.altamirapress.com

PO Box 317, Oxford, OX2 9RU, UK

British Library Cataloguing in Publication Information Available

Library of Congress Cataloguing-in-Publication Data

Brophy, Sarah S., 1961-
  Is your museum grant-ready? : assessing your organization's potential for
funding / Sarah S. Brophy.
      p. cm. — (American Association for State and Local History book series)
  Includes bibliographical references and index.
  ISBN 0-7591-0650-9 (cloth : alk. paper) — ISBN 0-7591-0651-7 (pbk. : alk.
paper)
  1. Museum finance—United States. 2. Museums—United States—
Management. 3. Endowments—United States. I. Title. II. Series.
  AM122.B76 2005
  069'.068—dc22
                                                                    2005009771

Printed in the United States of America

∞™ The paper used in this publication meets the minimum requirements
of American National Standard for Information Sciences—Permanence of
Paper for Printed Library Materials, ANSI/NISO Z39.48-1992.

Contents

Illustrations and Tables

ILLUSTRATIONS

TABLES

Acknowledgments

Over twenty years as student, staff member, and consultant at various institutions, during service in a variety of professional associations, and simply by attending many meetings, I thought I had met a lot of museum folk. I was pleased to come to know many more while writing this book. Thus, half of those in the following list are new friends, while the other half are people I have worked with, or begged advice from, before. I thank them all for their willingness to speak with me, provide examples and advice for the book, and review chapters. They are all quite good sports.

INSTITUTIONS

American Association for State and Local History, TN, Terry Davis

Bell County Historical Society, KY, Sam May
Blithewold Mansion, Gardens, and Arboretum, RI, Eric Hertfelder
Job Carr Cabin Museum, WA, Pat Seaman
Ben B. Cheney Foundation, WA, Ken Ristine
Conner Prairie, IN, Cinda Baldwin and JiaYi Chan
George F. and Sybil H. Fuller Foundation, MA, David Hallock
Georgetown Society, Inc., CO, Ronald Neely and his staff
Marblehead Historical Society, MA, Judy Anderson
Minnesota Historical Society, MN, David Grabitske, Carol Schreider, and Jennifer Lanning
Paul Revere Memorial Association, MA, Nina Zannieri
Prince Charitable Trusts, Rhode Island Grants Program, DC and IL, Kristin Pauly
Nina Mason Pulliam Charitable Trust, IN, Michael Twyman
Sandwich Glass Museum, MA, Bruce Courson
Scott County Historical Society, MN, John Gutteter
Thurber House, OH, Emily Swartzlander
Tsongas Industrial History Center, MA, Peter Savage O'Connell
Webb-Deane-Stevens Museum, CT, Jennifer Eifrig

MUSEUM AND FOUNDATION PROFESSIONALS

Adjoa Acquaah-Harrison, Paragon Group International, MA, and WingSpan International NGO, Ghana, West Africa.
Minda Borun, The Franklin Institute Science Museum, PA
Joan Benedetto, copy editor, MA
Dorothy Chen-Courtin, public relations and marketing consultant, MA
Manda Gifford, Coastal Museums, Canterbury, England
Elizabeth Heile, Philanthropy Communications Group, WA

Dorrie Bonner Kehoe, education consultant, MA
Laura Roberts, management consultant to cultural nonprofits, MA
Tony Silbert of Silbert Consulting Services, CA
Stephanie Upton, museum consultant, MA
Michael Wyland, Sumption and Wyland, SD
Sally Zinno, financial consultant to nonprofits, RI

Long ago, Hope Alswang taught me how "money must do more than one thing."

To Ken Ristine I owe the articulation of the concept "convince the funder of the need, and then of your appropriateness to *fulfill* that need."

Laura Roberts is my management and planning guru, and a staunch defender of the faith: "Every project should contribute to the organization's strategic objectives."

Stephanie Upton is a long-time, valued colleague, friend, and advisor.

Sally Zinno, management and financial consultant to arts and cultural organizations, is my budgeting guru. She provided the *entire* section on assessing financial stability in chapter 5 based on her 25-plus years of consulting, training, and hands-on management experience in museums, arts, and cultural organizations, and other nonprofit institutions.

To the AltaMira Press staff, spread out in all sorts of places around the United States, I owe great thanks. Their positive attitudes and communication skills made this so much easier.

Introduction:
Are You There Yet?

It's a threshold moment when your organization crosses that line between "good" and "fundable." You will feel it one day as a number of successes coincide: The annual appeal surpasses its goal, your attendance grows well for the second year running, and the flagship education program attracts a community service award. That is when you move from asking only friends and family for gifts to approaching other institutions—foundations.

Whether or not you are really "there," though, is something too few institutions have thoughtfully considered. Yes, you have probably evaluated yourself based on the field standards—mission, management, staff, programs, and collections—but remember, the field will not be funding you. You are asking institutions to fund you, so evaluate your readiness from a foundation's point of view:

- Do you do something important?
- Do you do it well?

- Do you do it for anyone in particular?
- Can you do it again, or help anyone else do it again?
- Is your organization a safe investment? A wise investment?
- Are you a good partner?
- What edge sets you apart from other organizations and their projects?

The growth and maturity of an organization has a great deal to do with grant readiness. Some things you just can't rush—but understanding what readiness is, and working toward it as your organization matures, will help you get there faster.

It's not a question of whether or not you can compete. You *must* compete. If you are to diversify your income, expand or improve programs, or broaden your reach, grant support is a big help. Even if all you want is to remain good at what you currently do, diversifying income and expanding your connections are excellent ways to strengthen your organization. You cannot shirk this work without putting your organization at a disadvantage.

Becoming grant-ready is an important achievement for an institution. It requires hard work, sureness of purpose, quality of performance, and excellent behavior—but this is expected of a charitable institution anyway. The first step in developing a grants program is developing an organization and programs that will attract funding. By assessing your organization with the recommendations in these pages, you can develop realistic expectations of return.

You may discover through this assessment that you need to bring some components up to speed before beginning applications. Maybe you will find that simply documenting what you do, the need for it, and its quality will be enough to get you ready. Better yet, perhaps you will confirm your readiness and can confidently commit resources to a grants program.

If this book tells you that it is not yet time to apply for grants, use the information to strengthen portions of your organization and your work so that soon you can apply. Chapters 4 through 6 tell you what to look for in assessing your readiness. If you find you are not grant-ready, chapter 7 gives more complete descriptions of *how* to address the important components—data collection, evaluation, proving your dependability and ability. The appendixes include a resource section for more information on these key topics.

If your assessment tells you that you are ready, then begin proposal writing, but be sure to read chapter 8, "Maintaining Momentum." It takes as much care and diligence to stay ready as it does to get ready. When you turn to proposal writing, you will find in the appendixes information on the proposal-development process and a list of recommended grantsmanship books.

Telling you what to do, though, is not nearly as effective as *showing* you, and that is why some chapters include case studies of institutions. These seven museums and historical societies were selected first for their grant-readiness and second for their variety of geographic location and institutional format. Though each is shown only once, there are references to them in many chapters. A good example for one chapter is sure to have suitable qualities that apply to the other chapters as well because to be truly grant-ready the institution must be performing well in all aspects of its work. Throughout the text you will find references to other historical agencies with qualities of grant-readiness; note, in particular, the mention of the Paul Revere Memorial Association: it's an example of a small place with big momentum.

The appendixes include a grant-ready checklist, proposal writing tips, and a list of my favorite, most-used resources.

A word of caution: Grants and grant programs are not for every organization. When you commit staff and volunteer resources to preparing a grant proposal, setting aside other important business temporarily, be sure you are investing wisely. If you wonder whether the application and reporting process for a grant, or grants in general, is too burdensome, be sure to review all parts of the process carefully before proceeding: identifying and cultivating the foundation donor, the proposed program's value and importance to the institution, the time it takes to write a good proposal, whether or not you can use the proposal material again, if the potential award is enough money, and what it will take to deliver the project and manage the grant.

Your expectations of return must be high and not just based on money. Certainly you should make a mission and program match that, compared with the foundation's giving history, suggests a better than fifty-fifty chance of winning the award. Be sure that the grant is for work in an area important to you and your constituents, and provides institutional advancement based on institutional goals. Resist the temptation to go after money just because "it's there."

Asking for money imparts responsibility and requires due diligence. It's their money, so the donor has a right to create guidelines; to convince the donor to give anything, you'll have to approach the project and proposal from the donor's viewpoint, not just yours. Still, the grant has to be right for you, too, so make sure you are asking for enough money to do an important job and do it well.

In my research I have enjoyed the generosity of time and advice from many funders and recipients. Rarely was I turned down when I asked for comments or material, and then only regretfully. I hope this book does a great deal to help you gain traction and then maintain your momentum. I am sure that if you, too, talk with funders and colleagues along the way, you will find help with whatever else you may need to be grant-ready.

Best wishes and best of luck.

Grant-Ready Checklist

This is not a score sheet. It is a checklist for helping you consider all the important factors when assessing your appeal to a foundation donor.

DO YOU DO SOMETHING IMPORTANT?

- Can you show the need?
- Can you show how your impact is significant and appropriate?
- Is there competition? Can you say why or why not?

FOR ANYONE IN PARTICULAR?

- Can you provide a detailed description of your audience?
- Can you show how they matter to you and to your donor?

- Why this particular audience?
- Are there others you expect to serve in the future?

DO YOU DO IT WELL?

- Are you accredited or qualified in appropriate ways?
- Do you regularly and conscientiously evaluate staff performance and program success?
- Can you provide award information or complimentary letters as third-party endorsements?
- Do you continue to improve your performance?

DO YOU MAKE A DIFFERENCE?

- Can you describe your work in terms of *benefits*, not *features*?
- Can you explain and demonstrate the difference you make?
- Can you explain why that difference matters?

ARE YOU A SMART INVESTMENT? A SAFE ONE?

- Is your mission statement clear?
- Do you have qualified consultants, collaborators, advisors, staff, board members, and volunteers?
- Do you demonstrate best practice in your field?
- Does your governing body have a clear purpose and clear, appropriate roles?
  - Do you have effective, up-to-date by-laws?
  - Do you have a personnel policy? An ethics statement?

- Do you have an interpretive and/or education plan? A preservation and/or collections plan?
  - Are you accredited or qualified in appropriate ways?
  - Do you have plans to remedy any gaps here?
- Do you have a charitable edge? Professional and innovative edges?
- How about financial management?
  - Is your financial situation reasonable?
  - Do you have an annual audit?
  - Is there an investment plan?
  - Are there guidelines for restricted financial gifts and for sponsorships?
- Do you maximize impact by replicating or extending the project?

ARE YOU A GOOD PARTNER?

Internally:

- Do you apply your mission internally?
- Do you say *thank you* for grants?
- Do you manage projects intelligently and well?
- Do you submit thorough, useful reports on time?
- Do you supply visual evidence of your work the donor can use for its own promotion?
- Do you maintain the relationship even when you aren't asking for funding?

Externally:

- Can you show how you behave well in your own community?

- Can you demonstrate successful partnerships with credible, important partners?
- Can you demonstrate your awareness of both your environment and your donor's?
- Will they want to fund you again?

ONE

From the Foundation's Point of View

WHAT IS A FOUNDATION?

The first rule of fund-raising is: Get to know your donor.

So, before you start to think about choosing a project and starting that proposal, you need to study your donor: Learn about the foundation's history and mission, whom it supports, who is on the board, how it gives its money, and what it likes in return. Each foundation will be different. A community foundation will have very specific geographic limits, and any foundation will have mission differences. On decision day, comments from the foundation staff may be powerful or absent. One foundation will dislike named gifts and avoid endowments; another will only give money for equipment. Each board member may be allowed a discretionary project, or not. Recent changes in board makeup may shift the giving emphasis. Then again, it may all go down to familiarity with the project and the people. You don't know unless you know your donor. As Tony Silbert of Silbert Consulting

Services puts it, "When you've seen one foundation, you've seen one foundation."

Before you begin your new foundation friendships, let's be sure that you are familiar with the basics of foundation types, giving styles, and kinds of money. Using IRS definitions, the Foundation Center helpfully divides the arena into private foundations and public charities. Each in turn is broken into other categories: Private foundations include independent, corporate, and operating foundations; public foundations include mostly community foundations. As the Foundation Center explains, both public and private foundations, whether created in the form of nonprofit corporations or charitable trusts, exist generally to make grants to organizations, institutions, or individuals for scientific, educational, cultural, religious, or other charitable purposes.

Private foundations usually have one source of endowment and contributions, such as one family's support or a single bequest. Every year, private grant-making foundations must distribute a minimum of 5 percent of their assets. The majority of private foundations are independent foundations, with the family foundations following along behind. Private foundations publish IRS return Form 990-PFs. According to the Foundation Center, "The IRS requires that every private foundation file a Form 990-PF each year. IRS returns provide basic financial data, a complete grants list, the names of the foundation's trustees and officers, and other information on the foundation."[1] These are public forms you can request from the funder, find online in the fee-based Foundation Center's resources, and often obtain through a grant-makers' association library near you. From this filing you can often determine a great deal of very valuable information: residences of board members (to check your membership list and determine potential giving affinities); investment interests that may indicate giving preferences or misalignments (any applicant with a mission of self-healing would not apply to a foundation earning its income from pharmaceuticals, for example); how much money is available for distribution and to whom they have given in the past (and in what amounts).

Public charities have multiple sources of grant-making money (hence the "public" in the name), including individuals, governments, other foundations, or fees for the foundation's service. They must also actively seek support from multiple sources to retain public charity status. Public charities publish IRS return Form 990s.

HOW THEY GIVE AWAY MONEY

Organizations may apply to both public charities and private foundations. The foundation makes all decisions about how much to give, to whom, and why. That's why many of the foundations listed in the directories can say "applications not accepted." These funders make gifts to organizations they already know, or to ones that they have preselected for pursuing mutually compatible goals. They are your targets for cultivation, not application; wait until you have developed a relationship with them and are encouraged to apply, no matter how "right" you believe you are for them.

No two foundations distribute their funds in exactly the same way. Each defines its special interests and giving methods in its giving guidelines. The foundation's funding priorities and interests may be few or many, and be narrowly or broadly defined. They can follow specifications in the original gift or subsequent evolution in the mission. Sometimes a foundation has a single focus—for example, historic interiors only. Sometimes it is broad—land conservation, historic preservation, K–12 education, *and* anti-sprawl. Call the foundation if its guidelines are not on the Web. Asking for print guidelines and any proposal forms the foundation might use will not commit you to applying but will provide the information you need to decide if you should.

These guidelines also describe *how* the foundation gives away money. The two main styles are responsive and proactive grant making. Responsive grant making, sometimes called reactive, is a response to unsolicited requests. Awards are made either as the proposals arrive or in competitive rounds. Each category of grants—arts and culture, historic preservation, social services, or scientific research—may have a claim on a set percentage of giving for that cycle or that year, or a category may claim all the funds for a specific cycle. Sometimes the proportions may instead reflect the applicant pool: If 40 percent of the applications are for preservation projects, then 40 percent of the available funds may be awarded to that interest area. If a cycle has a large number of particularly competitive educational programming initiatives, the staff or the board may feel free to award more money in that area this time. They may or may not compensate with a financial shift in a later round. It is their money, and they decide how to decide. Since methods and priorities continually evolve within the organization, the print materials may not tell the whole story. Talk with the foundation staff about current interests and how giving decisions are made, and renew this conversation each time you apply.

Proactive grant making uses many tools for distributing money: scholarships and special awards to artists or promising professionals, requests for proposals (RFPs) on specific topics, and program-related investments designed to stimulate capital returns. RFPs are a tool for mature foundations experienced in a particular area of need and for those that want to tightly focus grant awards either periodically or year-round. Foundation staff and leaders learn so much over years of proposal reading, site visits, and fieldwork that they develop a sense of what can best be achieved and through which means. By focusing their resources on these efforts, they use their learning to increase the difference they make. RFPs help foundations maximize financial and mission impact. They also hold the recipient to a more specific standard of performance. Foundation officer Ken Ristine explains: "The push toward outcomes goes hand in hand with RFPs." The funder defines outcomes, or at least creates desirable categories for them, by issuing RFPs.

The Boston and San Francisco Foundations, both community foundations, use responsive grant making *and* RFPs. Their RFPs define a specific need or problem the foundation wishes to address—lack of marketing training for staff at cultural destinations, for example. They also identify desirable methods and results, and they request proposals from any organizations believing they have the solution. This limits the number of proposal submissions, which certainly helps foundation staff manage their time; but, more importantly, RFPs attract more competitive proposals. Good exposure can go a long way. Sometimes the applicants not successful in one round will be recommended for discretionary funds at the community foundation—funds given to, or created by, the foundation that the staff and board may use as they wish. The foundation's responsive deadlines allow them to fund institutions outside the RFP priorities but still within their mission.

KINDS OF MONEY

Foundation money is not the first money you are going to raise. "Family" money comes first—and family includes the board, staff, members, and users. The next ring of donors is the community with its businesses, clubs, and general interest donors. *Then* come the foundations. For example, the Ben B. Cheney Foundation focuses its giving first geographically and then by the applicants' promises of service to the community. Foundation officer Ken Ristine says that for the Cheney Foundation, "Due to proximity, the local organizations get an advantage in that we are willing to invest based upon plans because we feel we can evaluate the reasonableness of those plans. Organizations outside of our local area need to bring more to us [perhaps 40 percent of a capital campaign goal raised] as a way to better evaluate whether the project has the kind of support it needs to (1) reach the immediate goal, and (2) sustain itself in the future." The funders farthest from your organization, physically and figuratively, require the most convincing.

Earned income, annual appeal, and special gifts, plus sheer creativity, must finance your first projects so that you can demonstrate the planning, public interest, performance, and success you need to convince the foundations to give to *you*. When you do ask, be sure the money you need—operating, endowment, capital or project funds, or program-related investments—is something they are willing to give.

Capital Funds

Capital funds are for defined projects of "bricks and mortar" (building something) or major equipment purchases (something more lasting than today's computers), but rarely do these grants support an entire project. The scale of capital projects often requires more comprehensive planning to complete and multiple grants for funding. For example, one major funder for capital projects requires planning permission, construction specifications, a strong individual-giving base, and a rigorous capital campaign plan to make your application competitive. Another major funder makes capital gifts based primarily on total impact—numbers served—in the resulting building and assumes you have permissions and plans. Some foundations will want to make the lead gift and name the building; others will want no publicity and prefer to be the gift that completes the campaign. To make your case, be sure you understand the donor's interests and requirements, and then provide detailed building and fund-raising plans.

A word of caution for capital gifts: Often they seem like excellent naming opportunities—the donor wants a name associated with the gift, as in the Sarah Brophy Research Center. Difficulties arise when the research center or the new theater needs a facelift in ten years. Does the original gift cover the cost of the new work? If not, does the named opportunity expire with the next change? Think ahead. The original donor and/or the family should know that the naming has a life expectancy, and both the organization and the donor should discuss and agree on the terms of the gift and produce a gift agreement to reflect this decision.

A capital grant is not about just buildings, but what a building helps you do. Be able to describe how you will use the new or rehabilitated building, how you will pay its operating and renovation costs, and how it will advance your mission. If you can't, then you haven't planned well enough to win this grant.

Operating Support

Unrestricted operating support is every director's and board member's fantasy. Unfortunately, it remains just that for most. In the push for measurable outcomes, project-centered funding has nearly eliminated unrestricted grant support. In project support, a donor makes a restricted grant expecting a specific use and a certain return on the investment in a defined amount of time. This is far safer and more predictable than an unrestricted contribution for general use. Unrestricted gifts express a significant measure of faith that a "non-family" donor is unlikely to have in you just yet. So ask for project money before operating support until the donor has joined the family.

In 2003, the National Committee for Responsive Philanthropy (NCRP) met with local, regional, and national nonprofits to discuss "the importance of operating support grant making." Here are three of the reasons expressed for funder's reluctance to give operating grants: "fear of failure," "infrastructure anxiety," and lack of "exit strategies."

Providing operating support, which is in essence an unrestricted gift, clearly makes funders nervous; so how will you address these fears if you are asking for operating support? Fear of failure, as defined at the meeting, means not really knowing whether the grant will make a difference. Counteract this by helping the funder understand exactly what it gets for its operating dollars: In return for covering half the salary of the educator, the foundation is supporting her work goals of continued program delivery to three hundred on-site school groups, development of two new learning strands for the new Native American history gallery, and a refreshed print and online teachers' catalog promoting program sign-ups and rentals of learning trunks.

"Infrastructure anxiety" means a fear of dependency; for example, if the foundation does not keep funding your educator, it is responsible for the future job loss to the individual and the organization. So in your application explain how you plan to fund that individual in the future: You are working with another foundation, a known donor to such projects, in hopes of attracting an endowment for the educator's position, and you have two major donors interested in restricted endowment grants that you will approach by the end of the year to support the Educator Fund. An application without this type of planning is too weak to submit.

As for "exit strategies," the funder doesn't want you to become dependent on it for any form of support. They want some understanding that this grant is not a promise of support for the future, and that a disappointing performance on your part would be a good reason for not funding your organization again. Set their minds at ease. Let them know you understand that the possibility of future funding depends upon performance. Make sure they know what your strategic goals are and how you will meet those goals. Then keep them updated. At the same time, as in the example above, explain what relationships you are cultivating to develop other means of support, from foundations or from increased earned revenue. Good reporting and a good relationship will go a long way toward developing operating support.

Endowment

Endowment grants are as difficult to secure as operating support because they *create* operating support. You are asking the donor to give you money to put away, hopefully safely, and then take from, as you wish, over an unlimited amount of time. You must design the endowment request to satisfy donor needs while addressing your institutional needs, but such grants require careful planning early on. Before beginning this sort of campaign, you must have policies in place outlining investment guidelines, named gift expectations, and management procedures for restricted funds. Be sure that if the grant includes naming specifications or restrictions on income use, you consider all the financial

and legal implications for decades ahead. If interest income is restricted to certain uses, can you reasonably anticipate those uses
in perpetuity, or is there a mechanism to compensate for evolution? For example, chances are excellent that you will continue
to need an educator but, to be safe, the agreement should state
whom to ask if you need to redirect funds in the future. Clearly
you must have a strong relationship with the funder to tackle
these issues successfully.

Multiyear Grants

Multiyear pledges provide great security to the lucky museum attracting them, but they are hard to find right now. Multiyear
pledges come either after you have established your ability to
perform acceptably, even laudably, or if you have a capacity-
building project that requires development over time. The
bonus is a predictable funding stream for the project. Sometimes
second- or third-year payments are dependent upon the achievement of the previous year's performance goals. This is a reassur-
ing safeguard on the first multiyear grant to an organization.

Michael Twyman of the Nina Mason Pulliam Charitable
Trust, funder of the Conner Prairie project described in chapter
6, commented, "Oftentimes our foundation will make a one-year
commitment instead of multi-year one . . . to allow time to assess
an organization's performance, as well as to contain future grant
making commitments that adversely affect the Trust's ability to
award new grants." Talk with the foundation staff about the appropriateness of a multiyear request before you ask; during market declines or other economic crises, foundations that have
made multiyear pledges may need to finish those pledges before
accepting any applications for others.

Program-Related Investments

Program-related *investments* are a recent, less-used kind of support in the arts and culture field. Often they are really no-cost loans, but sometimes they provide money for a program that will generate income either to return to the donor or to reinvest in the next stage of the project. The project and timeframe will be very specific. Business plans and contracts accompany this sort of "grant." Usually the participating organizations know each other well before starting this process. By now I'm sure you realize that grants are born in a good donor relationship.

Funders will have distinct preferences for, or aversions to, types of funding: operating, multi-year, capital, and endowment. Please do not try to convert them. Determine their preferences and then fulfill them legitimately, or leave them alone.

FOUNDATIONS' GIVING INTERESTS

The foundation guidelines will explain where it prefers to give money. Resist temptation: Do not interpret giving interests broadly; do not reshape your project to fit their mission; do not create a project to fit their mission. Foundations receive *far* more proposals than they can fund. Any application even slightly outside the mission focus is rarely considered. Those with just a whiff of contrivance will be rejected. Your project and institution, and their mission and methods, must match at every level. Some of those levels may not be obvious to you. By calling before you apply, you can determine if replacing the 1830s windows violates their preservation principles. The change will make the house watertight, but is the removal something they can support? Another foundation may cite combating sprawl as a priority, but they may prefer to fund community awareness and staff training instead of rehabilitating downtown buildings. A careful review of the foundation's Form 990 or annual reports will list other funded projects that may highlight some important ingredients and some differences.

CONCLUSION

Remember to look beyond getting cash for your organization or project to the overall responsibility of continually marshalling resources to offer quality programs and resources for all your audiences. That is the hallmark of a worthy organization.

Grant readiness is a measure of institutional effectiveness in terms the funders value. In chapters 4–6 we'll review in more detail what that worthiness is, but first let's work on understanding how to develop a relationship with the funder.

NOTE

1. The Foundation Center. Learning Lab page, Frequently Asked Questions, www.fdncenter.org.

TWO

Developing Relationships

Now that you understand foundations, be sure they understand you. The rule that "people give to people" still applies from foundation to institution. Developing a lasting relationship with funders requires dedicated effort, combining outreach and research to build a connection. There are so many history museums and historical societies, for example, that without some advice, funders will find it difficult to know which groups and projects are the right ones to support. You must advise them. Your proposal will be only one step in that process, and definitely not the first. Spend as much or more time cultivating and educating the donor as you do researching, preparing, and submitting that proposal.

In fall of 2003, the *Boston Globe* asked the Foundation Center to survey the giving records of the one thousand largest U.S. foundations. The results illustrate the great amounts of money going to the largest institutions of higher education and the major museums and symphony orchestras. Authors Marcella Bombardieri and Walter V. Robinson highlighted two issues of importance in their discoveries: (a) smaller organizations have fewer resources and connections to attract funding, and (b) members of foundation boards give to people and places they know. The preponderance of substantial gifts to large institutions "leaves tens of thousands of other nonprofits . . . trying to out shout one another for remaining grant dollars." In the *Globe* article Michael Rodin, director of Foundation Fundraising at Columbia University, commented that his university "aims for 'total relationship management.'" He concedes that small nonprofits do not have "the budget, staff, or training to achieve anything like 'total relationship management,'" but explains that his organization and any other in the grant game must determine whom they might know at the target foundations and how their interests and goals intersect. You need not be relegated to out-shouting one another. Invest in those all-important relationships.

Donor cultivation—deliberate or otherwise—is just as important in grants fund-raising as in individual giving. Make sure the funder knows enough about you to be interested in you. Dorothy Chen-Courtin, a marketing consultant to nonprofits, says the "absolute requisite for interest is engagement." As you can see in the case example in this chapter for the Job Carr Cabin Museum and in the case in chapter 6 for the Westborough Historical Commission, the interest and understanding of a foundation board member early on can be very important, but there are many ways to create a relationship with the funder before you ask for support. Judy Anderson, curator of the Marblehead Museum and Historical Society in Massachusetts, scanned the list of board members at her target foundation and realized that she had known and had professional contact with two of them several years before. By calling to renew that relationship, she began a conversation about her aspirations for restoration and conservation work at the Jeremiah Lee Mansion. When the foundation received her written proposal, they knew all about her and her organization's plans for the house. She had strengthened her case by matching the board members' areas of interests with her project's goals, and so secured a multiyear gift, larger than she might have otherwise received had she not cultivated the relationship and tailored the proposal.

HOW TO MEET A DONOR

Research

Getting to know foundation officers is easier than you may realize. Start with good research. Those skills you and your staff have developed for uncovering and interpreting history translate beautifully into donor research. By using online and print resources, find your donors and as much public information as you can. Grant-makers libraries and the Foundation Center's cooperating libraries have these resources and provide training for using them. Your local reference librarian can help as well. Read two or three years of a funder's IRS Form 990-PFs or 990s for information on investments, assets, changes in value, trustee addresses, and that year's contributions. Back in your own office, use the Web to find out about organizations that won awards; consider talking with some for advice. This is when you may find that their award was a once-only gift, outside foundation guidelines, because of a personal relationship—good information.

Search the Web for additional information about the foundation and its trustees and donors in the news or in field periodicals. How well did their businesses and investments do last year? Have their contributions changed in any way that indicates increased or decreased giving ability in this year? There is no end to the research possibilities, so establish a minimum expectation for research on any target foundation and add to it when you can. If you don't have or can't afford access to online databases or print reference books, and you don't have a cooperating collection of the Foundation Center near you, ask a colleague at a private school or university if you can spend some time in their library. Outside the library, read newspapers, listen to the radio, and visit other institutions (not just historical ones) to collect leads and donor lists and to pick up on foundation activities and foundation trustee backgrounds and business. Add this information to your growing funder files.

Enlist others in your research. Nurture the philosophy with your board and staff that donor cultivation is a very important activity for everyone. At each board meeting, circulate lists of staff and board members at target foundations. If your board members recognize any names, they may be the best initial contact. Set deadlines for making these contacts *before* the next board meeting so your cultivation process moves purposefully. You may identify future opportunities: folks to begin inviting to programs or to join an advisory board, or connections that must wait until your board member and the funder's board member meet again next summer at the lakes. Board members and other volunteers who do not have foundation contacts can help out by writing appropriate letters in support of proposals and getting to know the staff and board members at foundations when they attend your events or if they meet at other functions.

Earning Introductions

Go to "Meet the Donors" events held by the local grant-makers association, and to foundation open houses or informational sessions. Scan the guest lists at conferences and gatherings and introduce yourself. Do *not* ask about specific projects, proposals, or funding chances. Get to know them, and then you can follow up with a hello-again letter, just a single page with an accompanying fact sheet and a newsletter or photo page. Hopefully the foundation staff will begin a file on you. Just be sure not to ask for money yet.

When you think you will be ready to apply for a specific need during the next six months, invite the foundation staff to your site for a meeting. If that fails, send an interim note with an update, useful information, or good news. Be sure they know of any special offerings you have that might trigger a reason for them to interact with you: conference rooms for retreats, dining facilities for special events, or study classes in an area of interest to them.

Engage Advisory Boards and Selection Panels

Volunteers who serve on advisory boards or committees for programs, events, or awards may help out later on in other ways. For the Thurber House's annual residency in children's literature, the staff asks children's publishing houses to recommend authors for the residency. An advisory committee reviews these recommendations and selects one resident each year. The publishers now know the house, the advisory committee knows the house, and the writers know the house. Now the publishers are willing to contribute books to be sold at the fund-raising Book Feast each year, and the advisory committee members and even some of the writers have become donors.

Ask Funders for Advice

If you are considering a new idea, perhaps a risky one, you may be able to convince funders to discuss the program and its fundability. These funders may or may not be your target donors, but should be ones who understand the work you are attempting and can advise on program design and implementation as well as funding. Any who become interested in supporting the project will let you know and may make suggestions on how best to apply. If they recommend other potential funders, they may be willing to make the introduction—far better than your cold call. In any case you have gained valuable feedback and contacts and furthered your own relationship with that funder.

Collaborate

In the beginning, you can build relationships by riding the coattails of other organizations more experienced in raising grant money. If you are part of a collaboration in which another institution is applying for support with a funder you could approach in the future, the experience will certainly bring you all the benefits of collaboration in general combined with exposure to a funder. If the application and project are successful, you can tell other funders that you participated in a collaborative project funded by the Mercury Foundation. At the end of the project, if you will not be competing against the collaborative's next project, you can talk to the funder about a solo application.

Use Your Events

You spend a lot of time and money on programs and special events. Put each event to work as a cultivation tool. If you have a funder you would like to know better and eventually apply to, invite their staff to observe a program or to just drop in during an event (but only if the free tickets are valued at fifty dollars or less so they can ethically accept them). Give them a chance to see the history fair, archeological dig, or after-school program without a high-pressure meeting. If they have seen you in action before you apply, their mental image of your work will be far stronger than one even the best proposal can generate. When you say goodbye that day, lay the groundwork for the next contact. If you asked a funder to support a special event but they said no because they are interested but unconvinced, invite them to the event. They might not have time for the whole event, so schedule your meeting to coincide with the parts you most want them to see. Perhaps you most want the funder to meet the performers or teachers, or to watch the students or hear from their parents. Be strategic. Explain the project and find out whether you should apply next year. Keep your ears open for what *does* motivate them.

THE MEETING

When you do get that golden chance to meet the funder on your home ground to explain your organization and its programs, Tony Silbert has some excellent recommendations: Get the right people to be part of the visit, and be sure to have an agenda to focus the meeting.

Silbert suggests that you

> include the fewest people it takes to answer all aspects of the project. For instance, the project director can speak to program design and implementation issues. The Executive Director can speak to the project's importance within the organization's mission. A development officer or "grant person" can speak to administration of the funds and also serve as the coordinator of the visit—making introductions and keeping things on track. Avoid symbolic gestures like including the Chairman of the Board or

clients unless you believe they genuinely bring information that cannot be provided by someone else.

Make sure everyone at the meeting has read the proposal, the background material on the foundation, and the biographies of its representatives.

As for the agenda, Silbert says,

> You may not stick to it, but being prepared with an agenda will keep you from returning the program officer's expectant gaze with a blank stare. Keep it simple: a tour of the facility and some time in a quiet conference area with the principals . . . have a "pre-game huddle" with the principals to outline who will speak to which issues. It's okay to ask the foundation in advance what areas they are most interested in or want to see. . . . Be sure to provide the foundation staff with clear directions to your site, along with maps and special instructions if necessary (e.g., construction site, wear sturdy shoes).

Do Lunch

Some foundations specifically say, "Do not prepare lunch or make other special arrangements." Sometimes, though, it's appropriate. During a major capital campaign at a southern museum, the director had Wednesday lunches in his office with local business leaders. The office table had four chairs: two for him and either a board or staff member, and two for representatives from the foundation or business. The routine was simple—meet the guests in the lobby for a tour of the museum and an explanation of the campaign; the caterer dropped off a simple sandwich/salad lunch that would be waiting for the guests and the staff after the tour. They all had to each lunch, whether there or at their own offices. Conversation stuck to the business, financial, and political communities of the city and to the campaign. The guests left with printed campaign material, and the staff followed up with an appropriate next step—a letter, an invitation, or a proposal. It was very effective.

Attend an Office Meeting

Not all funders encourage meetings on or off-site. Be very respectful of the staff's busy schedule. If you *are* invited to the office, the same rules apply as with the site meeting, but keep the meeting to a half-hour unless you are offered more. The same cast of characters should attend, and have that agenda in mind. Of course, be prepared, concise, confident, and professional. Leave behind something for their files that, in a page or so, describes you and leaves a visual record of your institution and your work. You may be tempted to bring a CD or video along, but don't. If they express an interest in a particular program, then offer to send an audiovisual sample.

CEMENTING THE RELATIONSHIP

Whether communicating by phone, e-mail, letter, or in person, be respectful and appreciative of the staff's time. Be clear and concise. To bolster their faith in you, show them you've done your homework by pointing out what you've learned and where you have done your research *before* you made this contact.

Calling before Applying

When you are ready to proceed with a proposal, and will not be meeting the donor beforehand, call before you write. One funder says call first "to avoid false hopes and disappointments." Most funders prefer, if not require, a phone conversation before accepting a grant proposal, so don't think you are inconveniencing the donor by calling. Any donor information that comes from print and electronic publications may be out of date, or worse, gathered without the donor's input. It could be grievously wrong, or just slightly off base. You could be applying for the right program with the wrong audience, or the right project and the wrong amount of money. In addition to all your research, the phone discussion with their staff will help you craft a more responsive and complete proposal, and it will improve your chances of success.

Before picking up the phone, practice your elevator-ride speech. This is your thirty-second sales pitch. Develop and practice it before making the call—write it out in case your courage fails you or your mind goes blank. Tell whoever answers: "I'm Sarah Brophy from the Landsdowne Historical Society. I've read your guidelines and Form 990, and visited your website. I believe our project matches your interests, but I would like to be sure before I submit a proposal. May I speak with a program officer about the appropriateness of the project and its components?" Then they know you have done your homework and will let you pass to the next level.

When you reach the officer, explain: "I'm Sarah Brophy from the Landsdowne Historical Society. We are considering applying to Riley Foundation for support of a community restoration project for our historic graveyard. We work with professional stone conservators to train high school students, adult volunteers, and the town's Department of Public Works in identification, assessment, and care of these eighteenth-century burial markers. Some 75 percent of the stones have suffered from weather and vandalism, and lie broken or buried in the graveyard. Our five-month training and conservation project will record and restore eighty-one stones, provide volunteers and town staff with training for ongoing maintenance, cultivate adult supporters of historic preservation, and encourage students to value and protect this site."

If you're calling to see whether the project is a good fit, say "Do you have time to speak with me about the appropriateness of this project?" If you are positive the project fits, but unsure how much to request, say "The project costs $35,000 and we would like to ask the Riley Foundation to consider $10,000 in support of this work."

Now that you have answered the who, what, when, where, how, and why, it's their turn to ask specific questions and then recommend whether or not you should apply, and how to apply. Be ready to answer questions like:

- Which of your personnel would be involved?
- How much it will cost?
- What are the goals and the outcomes?
- Can you replicate it?
- Would it be better done with a partner?
- Has anyone else done this? (Why or why not?)
- Why are you the best to do this?
- If it involves construction, do you have all the permits needed, start and end dates, estimated amounts, any contingency fund, and estimates of what you will need to borrow?
- Who else are you asking to support you?

It's okay to ask the funder how competitive the project might be. They'll explain that every pool is different, but that generally this type of project scores well (or does not). They have no time to waste reading ill-fitting proposals so they will give you a fair answer. If the answer is "You are certainly welcome to apply, but . . . ," don't apply. If they encourage you to apply, confirm any deadline dates and the proper contact information.

Remember to say thank you.

Foundation officers and government program directors are in the business of finding good ways to share their wealth. They want the best matches possible. Your intelligent, efficient presentation is an excellent introduction for your organization. Even if this project doesn't work out, you may collect excellent clues for your next approach. Your professionalism will be appreciated and will help you next time you call.

DURING CONSIDERATION

During the call, you can ask if you should send any updates while the application is being considered. Some donors will say no quite clearly. Others welcome copies of press releases, news articles, funding successes, building permits, and progress photographs. Always avoid annoying a donor, but do send pertinent material—particularly if it affects the project under consideration. An e-mail or phone message saying that you are mailing a copy of the Historic District Commission's yes vote is enough to make your point and to make sure they get the letter into the right grant file.

IF YOU RECEIVE A GRANT

Recognition

There is no substitute for thank you, but there are varieties. It's important to know which form of donor recognition is best for each donor. Every donor should receive a very prompt thank you letter from the director and another from at least one board member. If the foundation doesn't stipulate appropriate acknowledgment in its guidelines, you should ask. The foundation will probably be quite explicit about the appropriateness of including their logo or name on any media or other products, and whether or not to mention the donor in newsletters, on your website, and perhaps on the plaque in the visitor area. If the donor wishes to be anonymous, don't let anyone (in the office or on the board) forget it. When in doubt, ask again what is acceptable.

Staying Connected

You can stay in touch with the donor during the grant period even if the donor does not request interim reporting, just be considerate of the amount of mail and invitations the foundation staff receives. Invite them to the project kick-off, if it's appropriate; send a photograph of the restoration in progress; send a summary of the builder's progress at the halfway point. Any contact should leave the impression that you are attending to business, not wasting your time or their money, and performing as expected. If there should be a problem (delays in receiving the cypress for the greenhouse, the need to replace an ill consultant, or discontinuation of a paint line), call to let them know what has happened and how you are remedying it; then follow up with a letter summarizing the phone call. This will provide a paper trail for you and the donor when you review the project at its conclusion.

Reporting

Saying thank you is only a small part of your responsibility. Besides good stewardship of the grant, good reporting is essential to creating and maintaining a strong relationship with your donor. Many funders ask for specific kinds of reporting on the use of the funds and the results of the project. Be sure to note these formats and expectations before you begin the project so that you can comply fully and intelligently. Some may want interim reports; others only final ones.

When the funder does not ask for a report, take the initiative and provide the information that you find to be most appropriate. In most cases this means a single-page summary with numbers and text that describe the program experience, plus support materials ranging from examples of students' work and quotes from participants to images of the program in progress and copies of local newspaper coverage. Give the donor something to use to promote itself in its own annual report, on its website, or in conversation with other donors. The report reassures the donor that the funds were used properly, appropriately, and successfully.

If you experienced different results than expected, explain them. That information may be as helpful to the funder in its work as to you in your work. Who knows, the funder might be interested in further support in order to address these discoveries. No matter what, do not fail to report on what you did and to thank the donor, again, for its support.

Staying in Touch When the First Grant Is Complete

The grant award is your opportunity to stabilize and confirm your relationship with the donor. Thoughtful organizations, and those wishing to prolong their relationships, don't stop with "thank you." Elizabeth Heile of Philanthropy Communications Group in Washington explains that grant-worthy institutions "develop and exploit ongoing communication efforts to actively involve their donors in the success of the project." Some organizations send a sponsor or donor notebook with photographs, printed material, copies of press releases, and the project report all together. At Conner Prairie the development staff offers funders many opportunities to see "their" program or activity either in person or by videotape. Corporate sponsors of Conner Prairie's Dinner with Santa program for members also volunteer during one night of the event and are part of the program—seeing the "happy faces" rather than simply reading about them in the report. Cash and in-service support for the same project is a double contribution.

In between funding, stay in touch with your foundation contact by sharing useful information on your organization and the field. Two or three times per year will do the trick, but only send information they are not likely to see in their own e-lists, e-newsletters, and professional memberships. Invite them occasionally to join selection panels and brainstorming sessions. In all cases, make sure the contact is relevant and useful for both sides.

CONCLUSION

You *can* have a relationship with a funder without asking for money. You can share information, see them at committee meetings or on other boards, and suggest contacts for them. You can ask for and provide advice. You can offer them your facilities for rent, or invite them as guests to your events. As genuine partners, you will both benefit in many ways.

The Job Carr Cabin Museum

Case: A Working Relationship: The Ben B. Cheney Foundation and the Job Carr Cabin Museum

The Job Carr Cabin Museum in Tacoma, Washington, opened in 2000. It's a single site, a replica of a small cabin, generously allowed free use of land in one of Tacoma's Metro Parks sites, but it is owned and operated by a separate 501(c)(3) corporation. The museum employs just one part-time staff member in the role of executive director, program coordinator, educator, fund-raiser, ticket taker—you name it. The museum's budget is about $60,000; it has sixty-five members and a mailing list of four hundred. In a community of much larger entities, the cabin serves an important educational purpose because of its scale. Where an expansive focus and larger exhibits are appropriate at the nearby Washington State Historical Society, here students can experience the scale and detail of life in a one-room log cabin. Its programs support the state curriculum requirements for local history

The Job Carr Cabin Museum, Tacoma, Washington. Courtesy of the Job Carr Cabin Museum.

education and supply a type of programming with specific value to the area's teacher needs. For families the museum offers a relaxed indoor/outdoor weekend learning experience in a family-sized environment. It makes excellent use of Old Town's park and is a fine draw for suburban residents. Tacoma Metro Parks has actively encouraged the use of the park and local attention to activities there. However, as is often the case with new projects, the details of the cabin's role in the life of Old Town Tacoma were not this well defined at the outset.

Job Carr homesteaded on Puget Sound in 1864, near where he envisioned a stop for the transcontinental railroad. Today the area is known as Old Town. Near the center of this residentially oriented business district was a small, underused park owned and run by Tacoma Metro Parks. In the late 1990s a buzz began to develop around museum and cultural projects. The planning began for building the Tacoma Art Museum and the International Museum of Glass. The Washington State Historical Society built a major new museum in downtown Tacoma just a few miles from Old Town and next to the restored Union Station. Heritage and cultural tourism was a winning theme. The Old Town business community began organizing around the idea of building a replica of the historic Job Carr cabin in the park, near the original site of the cabin. The campaigners felt strongly that this was a chance for a major city like Tacoma to have a replica of the building that started the city. Much to their luck, Job Carr's descendants still lived nearby and would be a symbolic link to the past.

As plans developed, community and business leaders participated in the discussions. One of the leaders was a board member of the Ben B. Cheney Foundation. Although this didn't give the Carr Cabin a direct line to funding, it meant that the foundation knew of the cabin project very early on. Foundation staff and the Carr Cabin board met to discuss the project, and foundation leaders were able to encourage the cabin board to think beyond the initial building product to how it would do what it could do, and for whom. Certainly the cabin would need staff and ongoing funding for all the work ahead.

Ken Ristine, an officer for the Cheney Foundation, explained that commitment to a project is based on "what the organization is able to do with our support in a larger context." First identify your constituency, then work with that group to create the project or product, in this case a museum. "Cheney support hinges upon the organization identifying its constituency and laying out clear steps for how it intends to engage that constituency." Where first the goal may seem to be building a cabin, it's really about what the cabin will help the group *do* and how it will keep doing that for years to come. The Cheney Foundation made a grant to the capital campaign to build the cabin and then a two-year grant to support staffing. This second award was based on an outline of a plan for long-tem sustainability. Ristine explains that the key features of this plan were: (1) a model for how similar cultural organizations locally and nationally generally find the resources needed to operate, (2) an assessment of the cabin's ability to attract and capture those resources, and (3) a work plan for an employee (hired with the grant money) to bring the organization closer to the selected model for sustainability.

The foundation was "convinced that the board of directors of the Carr Cabin Museum really took to heart the process of achieving sustainability. One of the greatest challenges for an organization to survive is that the board of directors understand the connection between what an organization does to fulfill its mission and what must be done to bring in the resources to sustain that organization."

In this case, the donor became an advisor in a partnership that supported a mutual mission in the community. Knowledge of the project early on, a working partnership, and finally belief in the probable sustainability of the program combined to reduce the foundation's risk in the investment and encourage the partnership to continue.

THREE

Are You Grant-Ready?

You may be surprised that there is a definition of *grant-ready*. Certainly, you say, a good idea and a real need seem reasonable proof of readiness. Not necessarily. Our world is nothing if not competitive, and so the demand for funds far outstrips the money available.

Grant-winning organizations exhibit predictable traits—ones that make them grant-ready. Chances are that your organization has many of the components it needs to convince the foundation donors of its readiness. You just need to identify these components and show your organization to its advantage. Be warned, however, that as competition continues to increase, the definition of grant-ready will become even more detailed. Get cracking now if you want to keep up. Your job is to learn what readiness looks like, achieve it, and maintain it at your institution.

The following chapters will explain organizational readiness and how to achieve it, but let's take a look at the practicalities of the grants process and their effect on your organization if you plan to apply for grants.

UNDERSTANDING WHY TO APPLY FOR GRANTS

Grant programs and grant awards are not appropriate for all organizations or projects. Never mind that the record-keeping and case-making chores are ones you should be doing anyway; sometimes formatting it all requires more effort than the cash award will truly be worth. After you factor in staff time preparing the proposal and collecting supporting materials, it may not make sense to apply for $1,000 or $2,000 or even $5,000. You may not get the grant, it may be awarded at a lower amount, or the maximum award may not be enough money to really help you move forward. The decision to apply is easier if you can submit the same idea to multiple funders. If you're already going to apply to one foundation for $10,000, then applying to the Arts Council for its ceiling amount of $2,500 becomes more palatable than if the Arts Council were your only target. The proposal can't be copied verbatim because each funder is so different, but there are economies when you can reuse a concept and information in subsequent proposals to support the same project.

WHEN IS THE TIME RIGHT?

Some projects just do not appeal to funders. They may lack impact or have the wrong format. They may seem useful but not necessary to the funder. Or perhaps they are just too normal to be worth the oversight involved. If the project is at all "business as usual," it may not attract foundation support.

Money is not the only determining factor when you're considering whether or not to apply for support. There are equally important benefits from beginning a relationship with the funder, such as placing your materials before its board members and thereby expanding your circle of acquaintances, and reviewing their comments on your proposal.

Sometimes it is worth making the application for too little money simply because success would put that donor's name on your support list. If it's an important project, you're already preparing proposals, there's a mission match, *and* the small size of the grant is irrelevant compared to the value of the agency's endorsement, go ahead. You must determine your own threshold for applications. Be sure the staff and board understand this threshold concept and the risks involved so that inevitable disappointments do not derail an otherwise thoughtful process.

WHY THE BOARD AND STAFF
SHOULD ASSESS READINESS

Assessing readiness protects resources and reputations. Those inevitable "no's" are the most basic reason for assessing grant readiness. The less ready you are, the more likely the funder's answer will be no. Someone at your institution who is unfamiliar with the process and the requirements is sure to think that the application was a mistake in the first place, or that someone did something wrong. Proposals are turned down for a myriad of reasons that have nothing to do with the applicant: a change in donor interest, a torrent of crisis-based proposals that appeal to the funder under the circumstances, or perhaps too many similar proposals for better known organizations that time around. You cannot anticipate those barriers to your success, but you can identify your own barriers and remove them. That's the grant readiness process and the reason why the board and staff must assess the institutional readiness to apply for grants. This self-audit, when conducted either together or with shared acquaintances, educates both the staff and the board about the common expectations of funders, the performance requirements on your part, and reasonable hopes for success.

Inevitably a board will wonder if the director's requests for yet another assessment or plan is really necessary, so use the grant-ready checklist as a planning tool contributing to strategic planning. Piggyback the checklist work with other planning work. When you find blanks on the grant-ready checklist, build the needed work into your plan. If you have no evaluation programs, set three pilot evaluation programs as your goal for the fall cycle and then expand in increments. Perhaps now is the time to schedule the development of that much-needed interpretive plan. If you discover weaknesses in your audience tracking methods, fix them now. If accreditation is a five-year goal, then you can attest to understanding professional best practices.

As you develop your organization's annual and longer-term plans, list the foundation targets. Check the foundations' deadlines and place their application deadlines appropriately on your planning timetable. Some proposal writers keep schedules of projects, deadlines, and report due dates on dedicated white boards or posters with sticky notes. Others have grants calendars on their computer desktops or on their electronic calendars. Just be sure to give yourself enough warning (six weeks to six months depending upon the project) before the deadline to develop a good program and proposal. Annual deadlines for major proposals like the Institute of Museum and Library Services' (IMLS) Conservation Project Support, state preservation funds, or the National Endowment for the Humanities' (NEH) planning grants can dictate entire schedules, so plan accordingly. Just remember, a deadline is not a good enough reason for an application.

Does your board understand its role in the grant process? The members must help identify possible organizational donors; support the cultivation process by participating in site visits or funder office interviews, using connections to further relationships, by writing thank you notes and updates; and exercise patience during the proposal writing and waiting process. A little help informing new board members of the nature of grant fundraising and their role in that institutional process won't go amiss.

ACCEPTING THE PROCESS

Before we move into institution-wide readiness issues, let's tackle some of the back office nitty-gritty as well as the time factors. What does your office need to be ready for? Since the income flow for membership is far steadier than for grants, that very flow and the constant income is what keeps staff committed to handling the letters, sending out the preprinted cards in window envelopes, banking the money, and tracking the totals. It's a system, and constant use keeps it in good tune. The episodic nature of proposal writing and grants awards means the grant-process engine can get rusty and neglected. Managing this process takes extra discipline. You must commit your staff and board to supporting and fulfilling this work diligently.

Managing Information

Can you manage the information necessary for preparing, tracking, and reporting on grants? Can you create a paper trail so that your colleagues and successors can determine who was asked to fund which projects; who said yes and who said no; why; and whom to ask next? Can you manage a grant development system?

Sure, you can add grant tracking to your fund-raising database, or create a whole new one, but what is really important is if you have the staff, the discipline, and the commitment to keep good records and to consult them.

So what's the system? To identify grant opportunities you must know the organization and its projects as thoroughly as every involved staff member—combined. With that knowledge you can identify needs and bundle opportunities into the most appealing packages. You will be able to identify the programs or projects with grant appeal and those that must be paid for some other way. As you go, identify some funders for future support of still unnamed or unscheduled projects. If digitization is on the horizon, consider the appropriate NEH and IMLS deadlines and slot them into your longer-range funding plans. If a particular funder would be interested in the project but prefers to be the final gift in a campaign, not the lead gift, schedule them toward the end of your fund-raising schedule.

How do you make sense of all this? You can segment the foundation donor market just as you do your individual donors. You segregate your annual appeal and special gift requests by their interests, the size and timing of their most recent gifts, and the frequency of gifts. Segregate institutional requests by mission (education, collections, or teacher training, for example); need (high impact, research quality, or collaborative community work); type of giving (operating, multiyear, capital, or project only); and deadlines (once, yearly, quarterly, or on a rolling basis). Use your strategic plan to map your work plans, then match the donors' interests, priorities, and working styles to your needs. Keep your strategic and financial plans and the donor schedule updated.

Keep your funder files as up to date as possible. It is absolutely critical that you know who asked whom for what, at what time, for what reasons—and the response. The letters, proposals, responses, reports, and cancelled checks should all be copied for the paper file and, if appropriate, logged into a database. Even notes from phone conversations are critical bits to track. The file should house the research information on the foundation, notes from the original conversation to see if the proposal should be submitted, a copy of the proposal and attachments, the response, copy of the check, project updates, evaluation information, the report to the donor, and the next application. It should also include copies of related newspaper clippings, press releases, industry reports, and information on foundation staff. Just as you create an individual donor file, create an organizational donor file—and keep it updated. The upkeep may seem time consuming, but it is important to maintaining an active relationship with the donor. If you cannot attend well to the supporting information, how can you have a knowledgeable cultivation conversation with the donor later?

Keep a global-view operations log so that you can track progress at a glance. Note what went to whom, when, and when you expect a response.

Table 3.1. Information Table

Date Sent	Foundation	Project	Amount	Notice Date	Response	Follow-Up	Report Due
8/15/04	Kellogg	Immigration Exhibit	$25,000	11/30/04	No	Inquiry & intimation of plans for next ask	N/A
9/25/04	Burns Fdn.	Immigration Exhibit	$10,000	11/30/04	Yes - $10,000	Thanks; invite to opening; copy of press release	6/05 and 12/05
10/25/04	Crest Bank	School Programs	$5,000	12/15/04	Yes - $2,500	Thanks and copy of press release	12/15

About the Time Investment

Many of your staff and volunteers will not realize just how much time is required for the grant process. It takes time to develop good programs, research appropriate donors, write a rock-solid proposal, and then wait for the notice. As an institution, are you prepared to plan ahead far enough to prepare a proposal well before deadline and keep that idea current until the announcement date? Sometimes, with an existing program and case statement on your hard drive, you can respond quite quickly to an unexpected deadline, but often the process takes six weeks to six months for designing the project, creating a proposal, ensuring approval all around, and submitting it. You will need to commit to and support the research, planning, *and* writing components.

Allow considerable time for planning the program or project. Make sure the staff, volunteers, and collaborators understand the importance and value of taking the time to talk and plan. Then be prepared to enforce the priority of writing ahead of your competing projects. (See appendix A for proposal writing tips.) Shorter proposals require 8 to 20 hours to research and develop, depending upon how much planning and writing is already done. Major government proposals can take 40 to 120 hours to research and develop, depending upon their complexity, and another 4 to 8 hours for printing, copying, and packaging. Show some foresight and planning by submitting your proposal before deadline. It saves last-minute mistakes or losses and your attention to detail and organization may be noticed favorably in the funder's office.

Now all you have to do is wait for three to nine months until the awards date! Well, actually, no. Don't stop cultivating the funder. Many appreciate receiving updates or special information during the consideration period as long as they relate to the proposal under consideration. If you win an award, get great journalistic coverage, or win a supporting grant for the project, take the time to update funders currently considering applications.

BUDGETING FOR GRANTS

Of course, the grant process involves financial planning as well. Many museums and historical organizations budget a general amount for grant income and then cross their fingers. That's fine if you delay the outgo to *after* the income, but many do not. Make your choice. Are you going to do the project even if you do not get the grant? Then include the project in the budget along with the source of funds to use if there is no grant. Are you going to do the project or run the program only if you get enough grant support? Then leave it out. Sally Zinno, management and financial consultant to arts and cultural organizations, recommends using a budget footnote or a supplementary statement attached to the budget for grant-funded projects to be carried out only with specific outside funds. She encourages organizations to prepare a multiyear budget alongside the long-range plan, include growth strategies in the plan, and pick the top priorities. Include a note and/or list of the projects and the dollar costs with the budget and plan. For those who like to see both options very clearly, Zinno says some organization use two budgets—one with the things they will do no matter what, and a second with the incremental projects and their funding added.

LEGAL COMPLIANCE

A grant-ready organization is prepared to be compliant. The most basic legal compliance is to be sure you have the paperwork to prove that you (the organization making the application) are a corporation recognized as tax exempt under section 501(c)(3) of the Internal Revenue Code. Nearly every foundation will require its applicants to prove this tax status. Many foundations do not wish to make grants to tax-supported groups such as city or town governments. Often towns with responsibilities to preserve historic properties address this through a friends group with 501(c)(3) status. Call the foundation first to be sure this arrangement is acceptable, and when the friends group prepares its application, it explains its relationship with the town. If you have yet to set up a 501(c)(3) corporation, the Foundation Center has advice on the process. If you have begun the process but do not yet have the IRS letter explaining your tax-exempt status, many foundations will accept official evidence that your application is in process.

The American Association of Museums (AAM) explains that its

> accreditation process is predicated on the expectation that each museum complies with all local, state, and federal laws, codes, and regulations applicable to its facilities, operations, and administration. These laws include, but are not limited to the following: the Americans with Disabilities Act (ADA); Equal Employment Opportunity (EEO); and Native American Graves Protection and Repatriation Act (NAGPRA).

Granting agencies, whether foundations or government entities, will expect your compliance with the law and with field ethics. This includes historic preservation, environmental protection, lobbying efforts, financial and legal accountability, and copyrights. Fortunately, the government and other agencies can be very helpful in explaining how those affect you. If you don't know already, be sure to do your research when you are planning your project. A single line in your application saying that you have confirmed with the Department of Environmental Protection (DEP) that your work at the riverbed conforms to regulations goes a long way to confirming your credibility with a funder. Enclosing the DEP's response letter strengthens the point.

MANAGING THE GRANT

On that glorious day when an award letter arrives, will you be ready to properly manage the grant? That means doing what you said you would do, the way you said you would do it, and then reporting responsibly about the experience and its outcomes. Many funders have particular conditions they expect you to comply with. The foundation probably explained these conditions in the application packet. The conditions may be, for example, a guarantee of a drug-free workplace and equal opportunity policies; segregated accounts for the grant funds; returned earned interest; a final report in return for the last 25 percent of the grant; or a reimbursement basis rather than an outright check. In all cases, be sure you are prepared and able to comply.

And remember, you have made a contract. You cannot use the money for something else while you wait for the program to begin and then backfill with other money. You cannot run a different project with that money. When opportunities or constraints dictate a change in the way you plan to fulfill the grant, talk to the donor. It's not your money, so if you're doing something different with it you must get permission. Many funders are sympathetic to incidental issues that organizations constantly address. Explain the original plan, what has changed, and how you plan to address it.

REPORTING

Grant-ready organizations are committed to conscientious reporting. It's easy to forget a report if you have a change of staff or if your record-keeping system is faulty, but it is unacceptable. Often the foundation will remind you a report is due or overdue. Attend to this immediately. If you kept a file on the program or project as you went along, and completed your evaluations as promised, the material is ready for shaping into a brief report—not as hard as you think—but if it's not ready, the process can take days. For accuracy and expediency, be sure that both the development staff and program or project staff compile the report and then share it with the CEO before mailing it. Through the report, your organization will earn credibility with the funder and strengthen its relationship for the future. This is other peoples' money. Commit to managing it as carefully as if it were your own.

MOVING ON

So, you believe that soliciting foundation support will be appropriate in some cases; you understand there is a proper way to go about this and suspect you can handle the institutional burden of being a grant-soliciting, grant-managing organization. It is not a matter of merely writing well, but rather of making a rock-solid case in your proposals. Building that case requires work on your part even before you ask the foundation for a grant. Now it is time to examine your organization to be sure it will appeal to funders and attract grants. Do you do anything important and for anyone in particular? Does that audience matter to the funder? Do you do it well? Will you be able to demonstrate the difference you make? Will you be a good partner for the donor? Will you be a good investment? Let's find out.

FOUR

Why Do You Matter?

Do you do something special or important? Does it make a difference? For anyone in particular?

Uniqueness is no longer enough to warrant support; good ideas are not either. Museums must fulfill a demonstrable third-party need, not merely their own interpretations of need. You must be able to explain how the work makes a difference and how you are best suited to do this work. Let's look at need, audience, uniqueness, and quality to articulate exactly how you matter and to whom.

NEED

How do you explain that you're doing something important? If it is important, there must be a visible need for this project or your organization. How is that need expressed? Does the frequency of historic home demolition in your area indicate a crisis?

Did the prison outreach program request a preservation skills workshop? Have you asked schoolteachers and camp directors what would help them most? Do teacher requests or the inquiry log demonstrate a need or interest area? Do your evaluations demonstrate a need or a repeated request? Can you provide external evidence of need from the newspaper, public comment, or polls?

Proving the Need

Perhaps the government can help. When many of the states began implementing curriculum frameworks for each school grade, historical organizations had ready-made needs statements. School district statistics on underserved groups can also pinpoint needs. When Conner Prairie in Indiana was developing a new outreach project through its *Follow the North Star* program, it used Indiana Department of Education statistics to identify underserved audiences. Some 63 percent of the Indianapolis public school students were eligible for free lunch. These free or reduced-price lunches are offered to families with children below an income level determined by the state. The percentage is a third-party figure a donor could depend on. The museum created a program where the foundation's contribution would significantly reduce the admission cost, while covering the transportation cost, to overcome the cost barrier for this student audience. The state's department of education figures provided a clear match with the donor's interest in serving an audience with limited access to cultural resources. (See chapter 6 for a more complete explanation of this project.)

Sometimes your evaluation work demonstrates the need. One southern museum, committed to teaching middle-school students about civic participation and the law, has a unique delivery style and excellent content, but stops short after delivery. The program is an excellent play, a re-creation of a historic debate, conversation, or trial. A member of the cast provides effective narration and then engages the students, or tries to. In the usual manner of school programs, some teachers have prepared the students; others have not. Not every teacher is prepared either. In most cases the whole grade attends at once, so three of the classes are chaperoned by math, science, and language arts teachers who are unfamiliar with the classroom discussion *and* are not prepared to coach the students. When the play ends, students can ask questions. Consistently only one or two of thirty students query the actors when they are in character. Ten are able to question the actors when the actors step out of character. The actors report that classes from parochial schools are far less participatory than those from public schools, but neither the actors nor the program staff knows why. This demonstrates at least three needs—preparing teachers and students in the subject before they come to the school, improving student confidence in asking questions of actors in and out of character, and researching why parochial students participate less. All can be the subject of proposals based on the need to improve the students' experience and their learning.

Many funders are motivated by community needs for access to cultural programming or quality out-of-school-time offerings, for example, but some are responsive to institutional needs in support of community interests. For the Sandwich Glass Museum, visitor responses provided external evidence of the institution's need for new exhibits that would bring return visitors: 77 percent of survey respondents were first-time-ever visitors, and 59 percent of them did not plan to visit again in the next three years! If the museum wanted to remain competitive, strengthen a learning source for the one million Cape Cod visitors from across the country, and improve its offerings for the Cape community, it clearly had to make some changes.

The Paul Revere Memorial Association, Boston, made its case for an institutional need in service of the public. For years it had been building its outreach programs (school, research, publications) as a way to grow without adding stress at its tiny site. In its successful application to IMLS, Nina Zannieri, executive director of the organization that owns the Paul Revere House, provided this summary:

> The Paul Revere Memorial Association will develop print and Web-based primary source curriculum materials, increase resources for teachers and students online, and improve the reservations system with a custom database. Together, these improvements will expand and enhance the association's educational services, reach families, children, and teachers more effectively, and streamline administrative practices. Given the space constraints of the small historic site, these improvements offer the best opportunities to significantly increase public access to rich and important historical resources.

That final sentence is brilliant. There is no doubt in the readers' minds that this project is *the* most appropriate for the institution at this time and that this, the association's highest need, achieves IMLS goals for its grant program. (P.S.—They got the grant.)

AUDIENCE

Of course, "need" is an audience-dependent concept. Can you describe your audience to the funder? They need to know who benefits from your work to be sure their money reaches the intended audience.

You must be able to describe the people and organizations you have, and want to have, in your audience. Identify your current users by tracking demographics at the cash register by asking for zip code information; by using sign-in sheets indicating origin by town, program, or state; or by taking periodic user surveys. Trap as much information as possible without burdening the visitor too much. Be sure to explain that this information helps you make your case to funders who finance your excellent programs and facilities.

Consider what categories make the most sense for your work, but imagine as widely as possible the types of information your funders will want to see. Find ways to describe your audiences in terms that connect with the funder. To describe visitors, you can start with basic categories like:

- walk-in visitors
- groups (school or tours) with name or source
- special events guests
- age (at least to child, youth, adult, and senior);
- ethnicity (not by verbal questioning or visual guessing, but if they define themselves accordingly in a survey they complete, or if the group they are traveling with provides this information)
- frequency of visits and whether this is a first visit (for the group or the individual)
- how they heard about you and why they came
- whether a particular event or exhibit enticed them this time

Then, let your audience describe itself. If you are with a group and you hope to determine specific ages or ethnicity, at the next meeting send around a sheet where participants can mark their own categories if they wish. When the "collecting family histories" course is filled through the local Council on Aging, the council staff can give you demographic information and teach you about your audience. Conner Prairie identified its audience using the Department of Education statistics on the students in Indianapolis public schools.

Thurber House in Columbus, Ohio, has a mix of ways, as you should, for creating a knowledge base of participants. Tour guests sign the guest book so that staff can track origin by city, state, and country. Using the computer program FilemakerPro, the staff tracks ticket orders for all programs to understand when a person first attended a Thurber House event, which events he or she attended, and whether he or she would like to receive mailings about Thurber House. This is the source for mailing lists and potential target audiences. Each year as the house selects a children's writer-in-residence, they choose a community service organization to work with the writer, based on the writer's talents and the needs of the Columbus community. With each new community group, the house gains a new constituency and a profile of those participants.

On the Scott County Historical Society's Web survey, one question is "How do you describe yourself?" All the options are based on ethnicity, a result of funders asking for proof of audience diversity. The labels "underserved," "socially excluded," and "with limited access to cultural resources" are attempts to delicately describe audience economic categories. These have real uses, but there are other ways people describe *themselves* that are clues to audience interests and needs. In talking with a group in the parlor, you may find an audience interested in women's rights, interior design, or even history! Your categories may include children without after-school care, students enrolled in English as a Second Language, immigrants, retired machinists, or unemployed technology workers.

How Do You Know What the Audience Is Thinking?

All institutions need to find out what the audience thinks. Peter O'Connell, director of the Tsongas Industrial History Center in Lowell, Massachusetts, explains that the Teacher Advisory Board is critical to the center because "the needs of schools and teachers continually change—especially in this era of education reform with all of its attendant requirements." Museum education programs without systematic mechanisms to gather information from their school audience may lose their audience suddenly and without knowing why. The Teacher Advisory Board keeps the center connected to its audience. Even with that direct line, other factors are important, he points out; the staff is committed to listening to teachers and involving them in many ways—the center's staff works with the school systems through a school liaison, by serving on curriculum committees in Lowell and at the state level, and by collaborating with school systems in submitting grant proposals. The center offers highly useful and usable tools of regular teacher workshops and easy-to-use curriculum materials. The Tsongas Center completely engages its teacher audience and uses that interaction to reach its student audience. Audience engagement is a contact sport.

UNIQUENESS

To prove your uniqueness or distinct value, you must know your market comparables. What are the other historic homes associated with authors or artists, presidents, or other statesmen? Are there other special-interest technology museums you should know about? What do other midwestern and western state historical societies do? What are their offerings? Who are their partners and their audiences? What are their attendance and their programming like? How large are their budgets? Is anyone else solving the problem? If not, that would help make your point. If so, then why are you necessary?

When Dorothy Chen-Courtin conducted such a study for the Emily Dickinson Homestead in Amherst, Massachusetts, she identified the James Thurber House in Columbus, Ohio; the Nightingale Brown House at Brown University in Providence, Rhode Island; and Evergreen House at Johns Hopkins University in Baltimore, Maryland. They were selected because they had a link to a literary figure and were owned by an educational institution. They gave the Homestead staff and consultants an opportunity to compare the operating methods, and the program and service offerings, of historic homes now used as literary centers, research sites, and special events venues.

When making its case to National Endowment for the Humanities (NEH), the Sandwich Glass Museum investigated the audience statistics, collections resources, and interpretive methods of glass-related museums and sites in Maine, New York, New Jersey, and Michigan as market comparables. The staff made the case that there was no similar competitor in the region—or anywhere else, for that matter.

QUALITY

Evaluation

Evaluation is not a new topic in funding circles, but it is becoming so common that no institution can get through a grant application without it. One factor contributing to the rise of the generic term *evaluation* was Congress's 1993 Government Performance and Results Act (GPRA) requiring government agencies to create, achieve, and report on specific objective, quantifiable, and measurable performance goals. For historical organizations, it means that many of our grant sources—National Endowment for the Arts (NEA), National Endowment for the Humanities (NEH), Institute for Museum and Library Services (IMLS), and National Science Foundation (NSF)—must require proof of results from funded projects to comply with the law. The idea has spread throughout granting bodies, including foundations, at the state and local levels as well, regardless of their association with the government.

You must be able to describe what impact your institution has on individuals. Evaluation takes discipline, but once the systems are in place and your staff begins to understand the real value, the work becomes easier. For those not fluent in this area, there is help. The United Way, the National Park Service, American Association for State and Local History (AASLH), NEH, NEA, the Kellogg Foundation, IMLS, and the United Kingdom's Museums, Libraries, and Archives Council (MLA) have great tools for you to consider. (See the tables from AASLH, MLA, and Conner Prairie in this chapter.) The day you find that you cannot make a decision until you see the evaluation material, you know you've internalized this important practice.

To be competitive in the coming years, historical institutions will have to describe their performance in ways that consumers can understand yet with tools that are appropriate to their business. Museums have few benchmarks to use, and measurement is more often done program by program, not institution-wide, or from the customers' viewpoint. Evaluation—or performance measurement, a better term—should be used to "increase effectiveness and communicate value." Evaluation shows that you are committed to doing your job well, not just getting it done.

Soon, so many evaluation tools will be available that the cry will not be "How do I do it?" but "How do I know which one to use?" It's the same for choosing a planning or organizational model: Take time to learn about the varieties, understand the language, decide what is important to achieve, and then choose the one that best helps you do that. Here's a quick lesson in language from the Arts Council England: "Evaluation is concerned with making judgments, based on evidence, about the value and quality of a project against agreed objectives. Documentation is about keeping a record of what happens throughout a project. Monitoring is a way of checking that all parts of the project are going to plan."[1] Table 4.1 is a description of the United Kingdom's Museums, Libraries, and Archives Council's Generic Learning Outcomes.

Museums and historical institutions tend to focus on the effort of documentation without recognizing the value of various tools for describing the quality and success of what we do. You can use the United Way's logic model for monitoring a project and visitor surveys to collect demographic information, identify advertising value, and determine public interests. For testing the effectiveness of an educational program or exhibit, you might choose the sequence of front-end, formative, and then summative evaluation. Outcome-based evaluation (OBE) can measure change in values, attitudes, feelings, and knowledge.

IMLS defines OBE as "the measurement of results. It identifies observations that can credibly demonstrate change or desirable conditions ('increased quality of work in the annual science fair,' 'interest in family history,' 'ability to use information effectively'). It systematically collects information about these indicators, and uses that information to show the extent to which a program achieved its goals." For IMLS, outcomes are "benefits to people: specifically, achievements or changes in skill, knowledge,

**Table 4.1. Five Generic Learning Outcomes
from the United Kingdom's Museums, Libraries, and Archives Council**

Measuring informal learning is very different than measuring school-based learning on tests: learners may not be interested in taking a test, and certainly can't be required to; and they may not even recognize what they've learned until later and in a different but related situation. In the United Kingdom, the government's Museums, Libraries, and Archives Council (MLA) has developed a tool for measuring what it calls "soft" outcomes of change in value attitudes, emotions and beliefs. MLA defines learning as "a process of active engagement with experience. It is what people do when they want to make sense of the world. It may involve increase in or deepening of skills, knowledge, understanding, values, feelings, attitudes and the capacity to reflect. Effective learning leads to change, development and the desire to learn more"[1]

The MLA's Five Generic Learning Outcomes are:
- Increase in knowledge and understanding
- Increase in skills
  - Intellectual skills (reading, thinking critically and analytically, being able to present a reasoned point of view, weighing up different forms of evidence)
  - Key skills (numeracy, communication, use of ICT, learning how to learn)
  - Information management skills (locating information, using information management systems, evaluating information)
  - Social skills (meeting people, being friendly, introducing others, remembering names, showing an interest in the concerns of others, team working)
  - Emotional skills (managing intense feelings such as anger, channelling energy into productive outcomes, recognizing the feelings of others)
  - Communication skills (writing, speaking, listening, giving a presentation, making a TV program)
  - Physical skills (running, dancing, manipulating materials to make things)
- Change in attitudes or values
  - Attitudes towards self
  - Attitudes towards others
  - Attitudes towards the organization
- Evidence of enjoyment, inspiration and creativity
- Evidence of activity, behavior, progression

These categories are flexible enough to applied to a variety of programs and situations and learners, and can even be used to categorize comments in your visitor guest book.

Note
[1] Measuring the Outcomes and Impact of Learning in Museums, Archives, and Libraries: The Learning Impact Research Project, End of Project Paper, resource: The Council for Museums, Archives, and Libraries (now MLA: The Museums, Libraries, and Achives Council), 01 May 2003. Now available on line at www.mla.gov.uk/action/learnacc/00insplearn.asp.

attitude, behavior, condition, or life status for program participants ('visitors will know what architecture contributes to their
environments,' 'participant literacy will improve')." Table 4.2
("Anticipated Outcomes" for Conner Prairie's *Follow the North
Star* program) is one example of how to describe what you wish
to achieve.

Table 4.2.   Conner Prairie's Goals and Strategies for *Follow the North Star*

Goals. Program support will extend outreach for *Follow the North Star* to:

1. reach new audiences, especially underprivileged audiences in the central Indiana region,
2. make the program available to a greater number of Indiana school children,
3. expand and enrich the participant experience, and
4. provide greater access for people who cannot physically participate in the program due to physical limitations or geographic distance.

Strategies. Following the first four successful years of this program, Conner Prairie has identified these goals below to further develop *Follow the North Star:*

1. The museum has identified target groups of underprivileged schools and adult learners who will be offered discounted admission or distance learning opportunities to encourage and support broader participation in the program. The Indianapolis Public Schools (IPS) will be targeted for the project as 63% of the students at these schools receive free lunch and this is a good indication of a high level of needy or underprivileged students (see appendix B).
2. Conner Prairie will continue to develop pre-visit and post-visit educational materials to expand and reinforce concepts presented through the program, and to suggest related follow-up activities to enhance the participant experience. These materials can be accessed on the museum's web site (see appendix C). Program support will also be applied to the museum's interactive distance learning presentations of *Follow the North Star.*
3. Marketing initiatives will be expanded to attract new audiences through print, web site development and e-mail communications.

Measurable Outcomes. The following measurable outcomes are anticipated:

1. A 50% discounted participation fee will allow broader access for area populations, including senior citizens, students, and underprivileged groups. Four hundred to 500 new participants will benefit from the fee discount.
2. Approximately 400 learners served by the program will demonstrate increased knowledge and appreciation of diversity and racial heritage in America.

Table 4.2. *(continued)*

3. By experiencing the historical phenomenon known as the Underground Railroad, participants will learn about prejudice and racial bias in nineteenth-century America and relate that experience to contemporary life, thereby becoming more thoughtful and responsible citizens. Exit surveys will be administered to participants to determine if they gained knowledge and insights from the experience that will be beneficial for contemporary life.

Outcome Indicators. The project will produce the following outcome indicators:

1. A 50% discounted participation fee for *Follow the North Star* will be provided for 200 to 250 students in sixteen middle schools and ten high schools in the Indianapolis Public School system during the spring and fall of 2002 and 2003 (see appendix B).

2. Distance learning opportunities for *Follow the North Star* will be provided to area schools, nursing homes, and church groups. Marketing strategies will be developed to target these audiences. Based upon prior history, the museum anticipates that approximately ten to twelve additional schools, nursing homes, or church groups will participate in distance learning broadcasts of the program in 2002 and 2003.

3. *Follow the North Star* has been presented to twenty-five church-affiliated groups with a total of 487 participants. In 2002 and 2003 the museum will serve approximately ten to twelve church groups serving disadvantaged populations with a total of 200 to 250 participants over the two-year period.

Crunching numbers isn't all of it, though. Changes in visitors' values, attitudes, knowledge, interest, and feelings *can* be measured, tracked, or noted with the right tool! It is not just how many students attended the program on the Kansas-Nebraska Act and how many answered 75 percent of the follow-up questions correctly during the bus ride home—did any learn that the Slavery Question was as much a political struggle as a moral one, and could they draw comparisons to powerful ideological struggles in today's world? When someone writes in the visitor book, "I never knew the cotton mill owners in the North were against the war with the South because they needed the cotton to stay in business," you have evidence of change, and it isn't a number.

If the funder is using an outcome measurement yardstick that is not appropriate for your work, talk to the staff about it before you try to shoehorn your work into their measurement methods. They may agree to your own version of outcome measurement, effectiveness identification, evaluation—whatever you wish to call it. If they do not provide a yardstick, provide your own—one that is appropriate to the work you do and measures the changes that are important to you: enlightenment on race issues in the 1960s, increased knowledge of midwestern states' geography, repeat visits to the museum by recent first-time visitors, development of long-term participation habits, or increased circulation in your lending library.

Evaluation is not just done "on" the visitor or "for" outsiders like grant funders. Evaluation information is critical information for internal management, for doing your job well. As United Way points out to its agencies, internal evaluation can provide direction for staff, identify training needs, and support planning, budget development, and resource allocation decisions. Do not let yourself believe it detracts from time spent on "important" issues like managing cash flow, promoting the institution, and working with the board. Information collected by measuring outcomes and evaluating exhibits and programs is part of the mix of information that helps you keep your institution on the right track. It's not just something you do for funders.

Those calling for more accountability in nonprofits are quick to say that the field should create its own yardstick or one will be applied to us—literally and figuratively. Enter AASLH. According to AASLH president Terry Davis,

For decades history organizations have been measuring their performance on specific aspects of their work, like evaluating what customers think of a specific program or exhibit, or measuring attendance. AASLH believes institutions should take a holistic approach to performance measurement, one that measures not only likes and dislikes and numbers, but value and mission. AASLH also believes this holistic approach to performance measurement should be an on-going part of business, feeding directly into strategic planning and the allocation of resources rather than to simply fulfill donor requirements or for reporting purposes. AASLH's National Performance Measurement Program uses economies of scale to make performance measurement affordable for history institutions of all sizes and scopes. The program offers assistance in areas of institutional readiness and root cause analysis. It's a program based on a cycle of first measure, then investigate (root causes), and then repair. Then measure again to see if the repairs worked. The program has the potential to change how history institutions think about evaluation and plan for a sustainable future.

AASLH's performance measurement program is a more flexible approach to evaluation. It measures more than outcomes, is scalable to even the smallest institution, and overcomes or significantly reduces the traditional cost barrier. (Questions from two of the AASLH surveys appear in tables 4.3 and 4.4.) But no evaluation tool will work unless it is definitely designed to complement strategic planning and the institution is ready to accept and address the results. And evaluation works only in an environment where there is honest inquiry, reluctance to find fault, and a willingness to use the tool regularly (making it a familiar and expected process).

The value of a fad is not the fad itself, but the opportunity and impetus to reexamine your institution's methods and meaning. Use it to your advantage if it is to your advantage. Consider the fashion honestly before deciding how to participate.

Table 4.3. AASLH Historic House Visitor Survey

Please tell us about your visit to the XYZ historic house today. We need your feedback as we continue to improve the museum. Please complete this survey and return it in the envelope provided - either in person or by mail. To assure confidentiality, the *Performance Measurement Resource Center*, a professional research organization, will be analyzing the results. There are no right or wrong answers. If you feel uncomfortable answering any question due to limited experience or any other factor, just write "DK" or "Don't Know" instead of an answer, and move to the next statement. We encourage you to answer as many as you can. Thank you for helping us improve the quality of the museum.

INSTRUCTIONS: Circle the ONE number following each statement that best indicates the extent to which you agree or disagree with it. For statistical purposes, some statements are positive and some negative, so read each item carefully before you respond.

		Strongly Disagree		Neutral							Strongly Agree
1	OVERALL RATING: I would rate the XYZ House overall as excellent.	0	1	2	3	4	5	6	7	8	9	10
2	OVERALL IMPACT: Visiting XYZ House has had a very positive impact on me personally.	0	1	2	3	4	5	6	7	8	9	10
3	DISAPPOINTED: I'm very disappointed in my XYZ House experience.	0	1	2	3	4	5	6	7	8	9	10
4	EXPECTATIONS: My experience overall was even better than I expected.	0	1	2	3	4	5	6	7	8	9	10
5	RETURN: If I were choosing again today, I would definitely choose to visit the XYZ House.	0	1	2	3	4	5	6	7	8	9	10
6	RECOMMEND: I highly recommend the XYZ House to my family and friends.	0	1	2	3	4	5	6	7	8	9	10
7	REPUTATION: The XYZ House is very well-known and regarded in the community.	0	1	2	3	4	5	6	7	8	9	10
8	VALUE: Visiting the XYZ House is an excellent value in terms of my time, effort, and cost.	0	1	2	3	4	5	6	7	8	9	10
9	PERSONALLY AFFECTED: I was strongly personally affected in a positive way as a result of my visit to the XYZ House.	0	1	2	3	4	5	6	7	8	9	10
10	OTHER HISTORIC HOUSES: Other historic houses in the area are as good as or better than the XYZ House.	0	1	2	3	4	5	6	7	8	9	10

		Strongly Disagree		Neutral							Strongly Agree
11	STORIES: I am extremely interested in the stories about the house itself and those who lived in it.	0	1	2	3	4	5	6	7	8	9	10
12	POINTS of VIEW: It is extremely important to show and tell history from the various points of view of everyone involved - not just the homeowner and his family.	0	1	2	3	4	5	6	7	8	9	10
13	ENTERTAINING: The way history was presented at XYZ House really held my attention making it an entertaining way to learn.	0	1	2	3	4	5	6	7	8	9	10
14	UNCOMFORTABLE STORIES: It is extremely important to learn about all aspects of history - even those which are unpleasant or might involve conflict.	0	1	2	3	4	5	6	7	8	9	10
15	TIME WELL-SPENT: Visiting XYZ House was time really well-spent.	0	1	2	3	4	5	6	7	8	9	10
16	CONNECTED: My (our) tour guide really made the history come alive for me/my family.	0	1	2	3	4	5	6	7	8	9	10
17	GROUNDS: The grounds/landscaping/surrounding area really added to my overall experience at XYZ House.	0	1	2	3	4	5	6	7	8	9	10
18	FINDING XYZ: It was very difficult to find and get to XYZ House.	0	1	2	3	4	5	6	7	8	9	10
19	STAFF: The staff at XYZ House was very knowledgeable, courteous, and helpful.	0	1	2	3	4	5	6	7	8	9	10

Table 4.3. *(continued)*

#	Question	0	1	2	3	4	5	6	7	8	9	10
20	WELL-KEPT FACILITIES: Everything at XYZ House was very clean and well-maintained.	0	1	2	3	4	5	6	7	8	9	10
21	LONG-TERM AVAILABILITY: It would be extremely disappointing if the XYZ House were not open and available to the public.	0	1	2	3	4	5	6	7	8	9	10
22	TOUR GUIDE: My (our) tour guide handled him/herself in a very professional manner.	0	1	2	3	4	5	6	7	8	9	10
23	TOUR CHOICES: I would really like it if I could choose my kind of tour (e.g. longer or shorter; emphasis on artifacts vs. stories, etc.).	0	1	2	3	4	5	6	7	8	9	10
		Much too short				Just right					Much too long	
24	TOUR LENGTH: The tour at XYZ House was…	0	1	2	3	4	5	6	7	8	9	10
25	custom q1											
26	custom q2											
27	custom q3											

JUST A FEW QUESTIONS FOR BACKGROUND PURPOSES.

28 Are you…? (Check any appropriate "yes" box.)

a "Member" of XYZ House [ ]   a volunteer at XYZ House [ ]

29 On which day of the week did you visit the XYZ House?

Monday [ ]   Tuesday [ ]   Wednesday [ ]   Thursday [ ]

Friday [ ]   Saturday [ ]   Sunday [ ]

30 About how far away do you live from the XYZ House?

Within 60 miles [ ]   61 - 120 miles away [ ]   More than 120 miles [ ]

31 About how often do you visit the XYZ House?

Several times a year [ ]   Once a year [ ]   Less than once a year [ ]

This is my first visit. [ ]

32 Please tell us how many were in your party visiting the XYZ House today. And don't forget to include yourself.

# of adults _____   # of children/teens _____

33 Into which group does your age fall?

19-34 [ ]   35-54 [ ]   55+ [ ]

34 Are you…?   Female [ ]   Male [ ]

35 Do you consider yourself to be…? (Check all that apply.)

African-American [ ]   Asian [ ]   Caucasian [ ]

Hispanic [ ]   Native American [ ]   Other: _____

36 What other sites have you visited in the past week or so? (Mark all "yes" answers.)

A [ ]   D [ ]

B [ ]   E [ ]

C [ ]   F [ ]

37 How did you first hear of the XYZ House? (Mark all "yes" answers.)

advertisement [ ]   article [ ]   learned upon arrival in city [ ]

Visitor Center [ ]   Web site [ ]   word of mouth [ ]

other:_____

38 What is the ONE most important idea or piece of information that you took away from your visit to the XYZ House today?

_____

_____

Surveys developed as a program of the American Association for State and Local History.

Table 4.4. AASLH Museums Visitor Survey

INSTRUCTIONS: The AASLH survey for history museums uses a 0–10 ranking system with "0" meaning "strongly disagree" and "10" meaning "strongly agree."

		Strongly Disagree				Neutral						Strongly Agree
1	OVERALL RATING: I would rate the XYZ Museum's programs and exhibits overall as excellent.	0	1	2	3	4	5	6	7	8	9	10
2	OVERALL IMPACT: Visiting the museum has had a very positive impact on me personally.	0	1	2	3	4	5	6	7	8	9	10
3	DISAPPOINTED: I'm very disappointed in how the programs I've experience have been run.	0	1	2	3	4	5	6	7	8	9	10
4	EXPECTATIONS: My experience overall has been even better than I expected.	0	1	2	3	4	5	6	7	8	9	10
5	RETURN: If I were choosing again today, I would definitely choose to visit the XYZ Museum.	0	1	2	3	4	5	6	7	8	9	10
6	RECOMMEND: I highly recommend the XYZ Museum to my family and friends.	0	1	2	3	4	5	6	7	8	9	10
7	REPUTATION: The Museum is very well known and regarded in the community.	0	1	2	3	4	5	6	7	8	9	10
8	VALUE: Visiting the Museum is an excellent value in terms of my time, effort, and cost.	0	1	2	3	4	5	6	7	8	9	10
9	HELPED BY EXPERIENCE: I'm much better off today as a result of visiting the Museum.	0	1	2	3	4	5	6	7	8	9	10
10	OTHER PROGRAMS: Other programs/exhibits available locally are as good or better than those at the XYZ Museum.	0	1	2	3	4	5	6	7	8	9	10
11	FEEL WELCOME: I feel very welcome and very comfortable when I visit the Museum.	0	1	2	3	4	5	6	7	8	9	10
12	LEARNING: I always learn something when I visit the Museum.	0	1	2	3	4	5	6	7	8	9	10
13	SPECIAL EXPERIENCE: I have been really personally affected by something I've experienced at the Museum.	0	1	2	3	4	5	6	7	8	9	10
14	HARD TO GET AROUND: It was very difficult to find my way around and get where I wanted to go.	0	1	2	3	4	5	6	7	8	9	10
15	CONNECTING WITH OTHERS: The Museum provides an excellent opportunity to have a memorable shared experience with my family and friends.	0	1	2	3	4	5	6	7	8	9	10
16	MY HISTORY: The Museum does a great job of preserving and presenting history as it relates to me.	0	1	2	3	4	5	6	7	8	9	10
17	MAKES A DIFFERENCE: The Museum is an important contributor to the quality of life in this community.	0	1	2	3	4	5	6	7	8	9	10
18	STAFF/VOLUNTEERS: The staff/volunteers at the Museum are always available, friendly, knowledgeable, and helpful.	0	1	2	3	4	5	6	7	8	9	10
19	COMFORTABLE ENVIRONMENT: The Museum is one of the few places where it's comfortable to learn about, discuss, and explore difficult issues in history.	0	1	2	3	4	5	6	7	8	9	10
20	MEDIA/ADVERTISING: I never see or hear about the Museum from television, radio, the Internet, newspapers, or other printed material.	0	1	2	3	4	5	6	7	8	9	10
21	TRUSTWORTHY: I always trust the information that the Museum presents in its programs/exhibits.	0	1	2	3	4	5	6	7	8	9	10
22	STIMULATING: Programs and exhibits at the Museum really stimulate me to learn more and delve into topics I might not otherwise have explored.	0	1	2	3	4	5	6	7	8	9	10
23	WELL-KEPT FACILITIES: The Museum's museum/grounds/restrooms are always clean and well-maintained.	0	1	2	3	4	5	6	7	8	9	10
24	"FUN" PLACE TO VISIT: Visiting the XYZ Museum is always a lot of "fun."	0	1	2	3	4	5	6	7	8	9	10
25	GREAT LEISURE CHOICE: With all the choices I have for my leisure time, a trip to the XYZ Museum is always time well spent.	0	1	2	3	4	5	6	7	8	9	10

Table 4.4. *(continued)*

JUST A FEW QUESTIONS FOR BACKGROUND PURPOSES.

26 Who is it that made the decision to visit the XYZ Museum today?

27 What day of the week is it?

Monday–Thursday   Friday   Saturday   Sunday

28 Today did you come specifically to see (mark all that apply)?

Exhibitions   Gardens   Libraries/Archives

Swan House   Tullie Smith Farm   Special Programs

29 Are you a member of the XYZ Museum?

Yes   No

30 If you are a member of the XYZ Museum, how long have you been a member?

Less than 1 year   1–5 years   More than 5 years

31 Please tell use how many were in your party today when you visited the Museum. Remember to include yourself. How many in your party were...?

Children under 6_____   Children 6–12_____   Teens 13–18_____

Adults 19–34_____   Adults 35–54_____   Adults 55 & Older_____

32 How often do you yourself visit the XYZ Museum?

Several times a year   About once a year   Less than once a year

This is your first visit

33 If you do not live in this area, are you...?

Visiting friends/relatives   On a day trip   Staying at a local hotel/motel/bed & breakfast

34 Are you?   Female   Male

35 Into which of the following does your age fall?

19–34   35–54   55 & older

36 Do you consider yourself to be (answer all that apply)...?

African American   Asian American   Caucasian

Hispanic   Native American   Other (specify)_____

Surveys developed as a program of the American Association for State and Local History.

ENDORSEMENTS

What about providing an outsider's opinion that you matter? Do you have third-party endorsement of your work's quality to prove that you matter? What is the public comment on your organization? Can you provide samples of supportive articles or news commentary? Blithewold Mansion, Gardens, and Arboretum has two powerful endorsements, one state and one national:

> Blithewold is "one of Rhode Island's greatest landscape treasures" and "by far the best preserved of the Ferry Hill summer estates."
> —Rhode Island Historical Preservation and Heritage Commission

> Blithewold is one of America's garden treasures. It is one of the best-preserved estate gardens in New England and one of the most significant collections of trees in the region. Blithewold is notable for its diversity of gardens and is gaining an increasingly important role in garden education in the region. The Garden Conservancy is involved in Blithewold in part because the community has rallied to save this garden treasure, and in part because Save Blithewold is putting the highest standards of stewardship in place for the next generation.

> —Bill Noble, director of Preservation Projects for the Garden Conservancy

When Barbara S. Hornby, past president of the Colorado Historical Society, gave Historic Georgetown, Inc., the Steven Hart Award for Preservation, she also gave them a priceless sound byte: "As Williamsburg dramatizes the founding propositions of seventeenth- and eighteenth-century America, as Mystic is to the whaling industry, so Georgetown and Silver Plume without rival can tell the story of the American West in the nineteenth century."

WHY DO YOU MATTER?

Conner Prairie's *Follow the North Star* won AASLH's 1999 Award of Merit "for a performance deemed excellent compared nationally with similar activities." The Bell County Historical Society's (BCHS) "250th Anniversary of Dr. Thomas Walker: The Opening of Kentucky" won the Bell County Chamber of Commerce's 2000 Preservation of History Award. For that same project, the Historical Confederation of Kentucky and the Kentucky Historical Society gave the BCHS the Presidential Award in recognition of the exhibit, certificates of commendation for the website and the print *Gateway Journal*, awards of merit for its computer CD project, celebration event, a school activities project, a new trail, and David Burn's book *Gateway: The Opening of Kentucky*. That is quite a haul—one likely to instill confidence in any funder.

Do not overlook less official endorsements, though. The local newspaper opinion on your building project or others' unsolicited public comments on your work are just as valuable to donors interested in the community's viewpoint as the profession's. The Volunteer Center of Rhode Island recognized Save Blithewold, Inc., with its inaugural Heart of the Community Award for "exemplary acts of volunteerism" in saving the mansion, garden, and arboretum. Sandwich Glass Museum used the local paper's editorial and articles along with senators' endorsements for its successful NEH Challenge Grant application. Just be sure the paper's editor is not on your board list. That would negate the ever-important third-party value.

CONCLUSION

Before the funder is willing to consider your project, they must believe in you—that you are doing good work, by anyone's

believe in you—that you are doing good work, by anyone's

standards, for a discernible cause and a legitimate audience. You have to do all the telling, but in a factual way. Save your emotional appeal for the concluding flourish in your proposal.

Now that you have followed Ken Ristine's advice and convinced the funder of the need, it's time to show them that your organization is "the one" to address this need.

NOTE

1. Sheila McGregor and Felicity Woolf, *Culture and Learning: Creating Arts and Heritage Education Projects* (London: Arts Council of England, 2002), 12.

Case: Need and Uniqueness: The Sandwich Glass Museum

The Sandwich Glass Musem

Husbands used to sit on the bench outside the Sandwich Glass Museum as their wives had a look around the cases of glass—blown, molded, and cut glass compotes, goblets, candlesticks, and yes, cup plates.

When Bruce Courson arrived as the new director in 1996 he suspected that the museum could do a great deal for the Sandwich story. The town of Sandwich and the Boston and Sandwich Glass Company were interpretive gold mines on the mechanization of the glass industry, the industrial transformation of a rural community, the ongoing impact of immigration on the industry and the area, shifting standards of living, and social stratification, the development of the union movement, evolution of labor-management relations, and the changing nature of production

The new furnace and a glassblowing demonstration at Sandwich Glass Museum, Sandwich, Massachusetts. Courtesy of the Sandwich Glass Museum and the Sandwich Historical Society, Inc.

and social relations in a national consumer economy . . . not to mention glassmaking. The question was, did anyone besides the historians want to see this stuff?

Courson began preparing the museum for change by assessing the public's interests. Information from the 1995 visitors survey indicated a need for change: 77 percent of respondents were first-time-ever visitors and 59 percent of them did not plan to visit again in the next three years, yet summering on the Cape is often an annual event offering repeated opportunities to visit the museum. Something was wrong. Typical visitor comments were "nice museum," "well-displayed," and "where can we go to see glass made?"

Courson followed up with stakeholder interviews as part of the precampaign planning process. The staff held focused workshops with scholars, collectors, educators, and residents, and conducted formal and informal surveys with visitors. Questionnaires sent to 508 members garnered an impressive 43 percent response rate:

41 percent would like to see a theater presentation
50 percent want exhibits geared to the more casual visitor (noncollectors)
53 percent would like to see glassmaking

Clear needs for the new facility began to emerge.

In July and August 1997, "undercover" staff members asked departing guests if it was worth visiting the museum. Though one eight-year-old said the museum was "awesome," the most common answers were "yes, if you like glass" and "yes, if you like colored glass and bottles." During that same time, front desk staff recorded seventy-one groups of guests choosing *not* to visit the museum because glassmaking was not demonstrated here. Members and visitors confided their interests: Why was the glass company built here? Why isn't it still here? What was it like when it was? How did they really make glass?

Armed with this information, Courson had little trouble making a case to his board. There was clear public interest in a renewed museum that re-created the furnace at the Boston and Sandwich Glass Company and sported a theater and renewed exhibits on the social, industrial, and economic history of the town and of glassmaking. Research also proved the uniqueness of the future museum.

All other New England institutions dedicated to interpreting industrial history and its related social history focused primarily on the textile industry. No other New England museum actively told the story of glass production. The Jones Museum of Glass and Ceramics in Maine had a collection of seven thousand glass pieces and no active interpretation of glassmaking. The Museum of American Glass at Wheaton Village, Millville, interpreted the glassmaking tradition of southern New Jersey with only occasional production for visitor viewing. The Corning Museum of Glass in New York had recently combined its glass center with its museum to improve interpretation, but without demonstrating historical glassmaking. Far away in Michigan, the Henry Ford Museum and Greenfield Village did have an extensive American glass collection and glassmaking demonstration program, but Sandwich would be *it* for New England.

So with visitor comments in hand, no museum competitors, and no industrial glassmaking buildings left in Sandwich, the museum could define a need and uniqueness for its expansion project—a major factor in winning one of only seven NEH challenge grants awarded to museums and historical agencies in 2000. The $440,000 created the momentum needed to publicly announce the $2.3 million campaign.

FIVE

Why Are You the One?

Now that you have proven the need, prove yourself. As foundation officer Ken Ristine points out regularly, you must convince your donor that you are the right choice for this necessary work.[1] Assuring the donor of institutional dependability and a programmatic return on investment means demonstrating a stable, well-managed institution that adheres to field standards and promises measurable results. Demonstrating your appropriateness as a partner will give you the basis for a strong and lasting relationship with the donor.

What will foundations look for in grant-ready institutions?

WORTHINESS

Foundation officers ask themselves: Does this museum do something we believe in, with appropriate standards, in a manner we can endorse, that makes effective use of resources for significant, needed change? And does it behave in a way that encourages us to be associated with it?

The W. K. Kellogg Foundation published "Building an Organization to Last: Reflections and Lessons Learned from SeaChange" in July 2003. It examined what had gone wrong in a particular project and what lessons it could impart. The writers highlighted characteristics of an organization likely to succeed. Not surprisingly, these are also components of an organization likely to be supported by institutional donors: a healthy financial plan, "clearly defined mission, good governance, capable organizational and financial management, and a plan with measurable outcomes."[2] The organization should have a mission and leadership that allow it "to adjust its strategies to accommodate a changing environment, . . . a realistic plan for action," and a board "sufficiently engaged."

That's a phenomenal list. Will you always fulfill all the criteria? An institution with momentum will. In the meantime, your job is to articulate what you have fulfilled and to address the balance. Here's an example. In its early years, Save Blithewold, Inc. (the organization managing Blithewold Mansion, Gardens, and Arboretum in Bristol, Rhode Island), approached the Prince Charitable Trusts for support. In summarizing the motivating factor behind the trusts' grants, Kristin Pauly, codirector of the Rhode Island grants program, wrote, "Blithewold has grown stronger with each year—and it is an organization that has covered all the bases well: important historic site, rare beauty; good management; dedicated staff; broad base of earned income and donations; large cadre of volunteers; well-organized fund-raising events; [and] serious horticulture and professionalism." Blithewold has almost achieved momentum. Pauly identified quality, stability, planning, support, and management as major factors contributing to its appeal, but not clear need, a defined audience impact, or a charitable or innovative edge—other components in achieving momentum. Blithewold continues to attract grants, strengthen the institution, and expand programs because it is gaining traction *and* has a clear view of what its momentum should be.

The Prince Charitable Trusts' support of Blithewold Mansion, Gardens, and Arboretum illustrates how an organization exhibiting the critical characteristics of commitment and ability inspire a connection with a donor. (See the first case following this chapter.)

RETURN ON INVESTMENT

Is your organization a safe investment? A good investment? In the 2002 report "Understanding Foundation Performance Assessment Today" from the Center for Effective Philanthropy, 67 percent of foundation CEOs anticipate increased scrutiny on foundations in the next ten years, and it's happening already. You can help them improve their performance by demonstrating your success, practicing economies of scale, and maximizing impact. Show clearly how you provide return on investment (ROI), and then maximize it.

Demonstrate Performance

We have already addressed evaluation, but this is documentation. Surely you can say how many school districts you serve, how many visitors come through your doors, or how your role with the Chamber of Commerce helped create a tourism promotion that increased attendance 20 percent during the "shoulder" seasons just before and after the major summer tour season.

Conner Prairie's performance goals for a project with the Indianapolis Public Schools were the standard for determining a second year's funding from the Nina Mason Pulliam Charitable Trust. The answer was "yes."

Maximize Impact

Money must do more than one thing.[3] Many foundations, corporations, and government agencies already encourage extension of a grant when they ask recipients to explain how their discoveries will be disseminated or how the project will be replicated. That is maximizing impact. Can you extend the value of your program by repeating or replicating the project, or helping others to do so? It is less expensive to reuse a program than to develop it, so either offer the program again, minus the planning costs, or help another institution offer it by delivering it at their site.

Multiple Goals

The money for the Historic Georgetown, Inc.'s (HGI) Gateway Visitors Center project definitely does "more than one thing." (See the second case following this chapter.) It provides services for a substantial traveling public, supports tourism and the local economy, creates a revenue stream for HGI, and sets "an architectural design standard for any other future development at the main access to the town."

In your case, "more than one thing" may mean that an outside lecturer should make a special training presentation to the staff when he or she comes to speak to your members and the public. You may create a collaborative training program that trains your staff and those from other sites, acquaints them all with local attractions, broadens their intellectual repertoire, and lays the groundwork for next year's multisite interpretive planning initiative. Funding for repairs may save you money that you can reserve for the conservation fund, and the project to rehouse the collection will train an intern in archival care and get the last part of your collection catalogued.

Share your discoveries with similar organizations in a presentation, report, or online newsletter. As part of the grant requirements, the town of Carlisle, Massachusetts, and the Carlisle Historical Society hosted a multitown gathering of town clerks, librarians, and local historical society staff and volunteers to share what they learned. The audience participants started two similar projects using consulting archivists to train municipal staff and volunteers—exactly what the Massachusetts Historic Records Advisory Board had in mind when making the grant.

HAVING AN EDGE

Charity

Still, these days you have to do more than just repeat yourself or multiply benefits in house. You have to extend the gift to others. This is your charitable edge. No, do not give away the money, but increase the foundation's return on investment. When the conservation center promises to offer its newly funded textile-cleaning lab to local historical agencies with once-a-month access and supervision, the charitable edge is obvious—the grant award serves multiple audiences. If the local government agency helps you bring arts groups to your area, are some of the tickets free or priced so that underserved audiences can attend? Set aside a number of seats for residents at the women's shelter or wards of the juvenile program at city court.

Invite Social Services to identify two children to benefit from history camperships this summer. Twice yearly you can share those grant-funded exhibit cases you had installed for your exhibits at town hall with other nonprofits between your installations. Invite other nonprofits to use your newly finished secondfloor meeting room at given times during the month. Allow other collecting institutions to use your new lab once monthly for the cost of materials only. When the annual barbecue event has outgrown the front field, share the event and its proceeds with the community parks program if you can fulfill the same goals for your institution and support the parks' goals. You can provide management and name recognition while the parks program supplies the site and staff to help with the work. The list is endless.

Yes, you could argue that the recipient institution is giving away some of its gift, but sharing your talents and resources enables you and others to do their jobs well and extends the donor's impact. The charitable action must serve the donor's mission, yours, and the second party's. Creating a management nightmare or waiving crucial or major income opportunities would be irresponsible, but if the benefit to other organizations outweighs the time it takes you to arrange and supervise the gift, you will extend the donor's gift, create alliances within your community, and improve services for more than just your little world. The more bang for its limited bucks, the better the foundation's performance. Think of the difference you make—and all you're doing is your job.

A Professional Edge

A professional edge is work of such quality and/or innovation that it adds value and new knowledge to the field. This is optimum performance. Yes, it's a difficult thing to achieve—but many organizations do it. If you want to successfully compete for limited grant dollars, you need an edge or two. Foundations do not have to fund anything less than the best or what they believe will be the best.

It is important to understand how the funder values demonstrated excellence versus innovation.[4] If the funder is a risk taker, it may prefer to see experimental work. If the funder has a reputation for championing confirmed quality, your proposal should offer a program with a substantial history and powerful endorsements. Most likely you can determine this by reviewing giving guidelines and the descriptions of funded projects. If you are unsure, ask the foundation staff. Remember, if the funder says that both types are important and you must decide, then the program that best supports your mission priorities wins out.

Innovation

Your professional edge can be an innovative program, process, or product that advances the field while serving needs in the best way possible. For example, the museum that has a teach-the-teachers tool demonstrably improving student learning and participation has a professional edge over straight program-delivery museums with no evaluation program. Your innovation may be finding new partners and new ways to use oral history in collecting and exhibiting information, for involving volunteers and new partners, or in collaborating locally, regionally, or nationally.

Why is innovation important? You may make the first cut in the selection process, and the second, but when the review committee sits around the table for final decisions and many components are equal among the surviving proposals, innovators will get the brass ring. Yes, it is hard to survive in the nonprofit world and have time to innovate, but many are doing it. Can you explain why you are not?

Your innovation may be in attitude, style, or method. Are you bucking the trend toward higher admission costs for new facilities by keeping a low fee or even reducing it? Remember when the trend began for curators to emphasize education, not just connoisseurship? How about when gift shops were encouraged to align their wares with the museum's collections and educational mission? These were once novel ideas.

Is your innovation really how you differentiate yourself from other museums or attractions? Have you incorporated audio, visual, or physical features into your exhibits in a new manner? Have you chosen an unusual focus for some of your work? Have you tested a joint admission ticket or applied jointly for funds for the first time? These changes in traditional behavior are personal innovations, not local, regional, or national. Provide some perspective so your donor will understand your innovation. If you have conscientiously addressed challenges with new thinking, be sure your donor knows. For many, an outward-thinking, confident organization is an asset as a partner.

Excellence

Your professional edge may be excellence. Is your project, which was once innovative, now so successful that others come to you for advice on replicating it at your site? As discussed in chapter 4, field recognition is as much a demonstration of excellence as evaluation can be. For example, many, many school local history programs are tied to grade-level curricula. Can you demonstrate that yours was designed and reviewed by people with appropriate skills and scholarship? Can you prove that administrators, teachers, students, and parents value this program for its effect on the students? The principles of defining excellence can help you articulate your professional edge.

DEPENDABILITY

If you want someone to invest money in your institution, can you show how dependable, stable, and sensible you are? In its publication "When Projects Flounder," the Ford Foundation identifies three triggers for floundering in grant-funded projects: program design, organizational performance, and conflict in strategy or values. Our discussion focuses on the second of these, organizational performance, when the "problem is not a grantee's programs . . . but the organization that runs them, which might face one or more of a series of problems ranging from financial mismanagement to high staff turnover." Signs of institutional weakness are chronic cash flow issues, a desperate chase for dollars, dubious funding breakthroughs, an inattentive board, and founder blind spots.[5] If any of these weaknesses are part of your organization's daily struggle, you have significant homework to do before being ready to prepare successful grant applications.

Financial Stability

Is your money management and fund development approach appropriate for the institution and the current financial environment? Can you demonstrate fiscal responsibility, transparency, and vigilance? Do you use your resources effectively? What is the rationale for your investment policies, fund-raising plan, and budget management?

Sally Zinno, financial consultant to nonprofits, explains that a foundation can use a museum's financial data as a tool for examining an institution's ability to carry out the proposed work. The following sections are based on her extensive experience with museums and other nonprofit institutions, including her work as a senior associate with National Arts Strategies (formerly National Arts Stabilization). The funder is interested in an organization's financial history, its ability to look ahead and project financial results, and its use of its own data or the experience of peers to develop budgets and program plans. These are signs of a thoughtful decision process and planning that promote financial health.

• What is the organization's financial asset base?

Most museums have either audits or financial compilations prepared by an outside audit firm. The statement of position (SOP), formerly called a balance sheet, provides key information for determining the assets available to the organization. The SOP classifies assets as unrestricted, permanently restricted, or temporarily restricted. The most important indicators are unrestricted and permanently restricted funds, and the level of liabilities or debt.

Unrestricted net assets are those that the board may use however it determines is best for the organization. To determine the amount of unrestricted assets that the organization can apply toward paying its bills, a funder can deduct the value of property, buildings, and equipment. A negative amount may mean that the museum is experiencing financial difficulties. If the value is less than 20 percent of the organization's operating budget, the organization may have cash flow problems.

The permanently restricted assets are donor-specified endowment, and some museums include the value of their collection. Key questions are: Does the organization have an endowment? What is its value, and how has the value changed over time? How much of the endowment does the museum use annually to support operations? What is the ratio of liabilities to assets? How much debt does the organization have? Is the debt short term (to be paid off in less than a year) or long term? How does the amount of the debt relate to the annual operating budget and the organization's net assets?

- How well does the museum manage its funds on an annual basis?

The annual audit or compilation includes a Statement of Activity (SOA) that indicates the operating revenue and expenses for the fiscal year, and often for the previous year as well. A funder can use the data in the SOA to explore questions about the museum's financial management, such as: Does the museum have a recent history of operating surpluses or deficits? What is the ratio of earned revenue to contributed revenue? How much of expenses support programmatic efforts? How reliant is the museum on any one funding source or funder? In general, nonprofit organizations are more sustainable if they have a history of annual surpluses and if they are supported by a diverse mix of revenue sources.

The funder can also ask the museum to submit copies of its regular monthly financial reports to determine whether the reports provide the board and staff with timely information about the status of the actual results compared to the budget and make projections for where the organization expects to end the fiscal year.

- How does the museum do over time?

Every organization's financial status changes annually, and even the best-run organizations have bad years. As a result, funders need to build their own system for reviewing the financial status or the grantee organizations over time. It is important to know the organization's own financial history, how it compares with other nonprofits in the community, and how it compares to peer organizations nationally.

There are good resources for securing comparative financial data. The American Association of Museums has published a financial information survey every three years with data indicated by type and size of museum. Service organizations such as the Association of Art Museum Directors, the Association of Science-Technology Centers, along with some regional museum associations produce comparative data reports. All nonprofits with budgets over $25,000 per year annually submit to the Internal Revenue Service an IRS Form 990 that reports key financial operating and asset data. Both data for individual museums and compilations of data by region or organization type are available on line through Guidestar (see the list of resources in appendix B).

Financial data are a key component of the array of information that the funders should analyze as they determine the needs and ability of each organization. Financial information does not stand alone, but it should be considered along with mission, value to the community, response to community needs, and relevance as funders make decisions about how to allocate their finite resources.[6]

BOARD AND STAFF ABILITY

What about the people who run and work for your institution? It is not just a matter of résumés; experience, attitude, and intentions count, too.

Board

We all know that an inattentive board and a founder with a blind spot or two can seriously impede the organization's ability to operate. A founding chair, or any other chair, uninterested in term limits or board rotation shows the donor that the institution is more a fiefdom than a responsive organization. The donor can expect that outside advice and information may not be welcome, that the status quo is more important than responsiveness to changing conditions. Be sure to demonstrate a healthy, working board adhering to the profession's standards.

Power centralized in a single person can be dangerous in other ways. For one midwestern transportation corridor project renewing a historic waterway, the founder's absorption in sudden financial difficulties stymied the entire project at just the point when momentum was building. The group had consolidated access or ownership of connected portions of the old waterway. The small museum exhibit at the extant portion had attracted local attention and support. Rail-to-trail, greenways, and parks design plans had been funded by the state and were nearly complete. The major local foundation capable of completing the fund-raising for the key working portion of the waterway had invited the board for an interview. The group could not and would not proceed without the leader. The meeting never happened; the proposal was never submitted. Future work with the funder is in serious jeopardy and the project has not moved forward.

Does your board have a coherent, usable structure with clearly defined roles and responsibilities? Is it clear by its behavior that it functions as a healthy board by recruiting and training its members, involving each one according to his or her strengths in fulfillment of the organization's mission? Is your board a true help in developing your resources—cash, capital assets, and personnel? If you answer no to any of these questions, you should be able to explain what the organization is doing to improve board governance.

Staff, Consultants, and Volunteers

Of course, it is not just the board the funder considers. The Kellogg Foundation, in its report "Building an Organization to Last: Reflections and Lessons Learned from SeaChange," explains that "a well-managed organization has . . . staff members who possess the skills required to effectively execute their responsibilities. In addition, a well-managed organization has a defined structure with lines of supervision, and clear roles and responsibilities."[7] Be sure their roles and positions are clearly defined and appropriate for your goals.

Do your staff and volunteers have the training, talent, and resources appropriate for this institution, and where it is headed? One reason many funders ask for an organizational chart is to help sort out some of these issues quickly. Be sure to convince the reviewers that you have the right staff in the positions and that they, the consultants and volunteers, are qualified for their jobs and have the authority to do them. Here's an example:

As a member of the founding staff of Tsongas Industrial History Center in Lowell, MA, Dorrie Bonner Kehoe and her colleagues initiated one of the first Teacher Advisory Boards in the East to help develop the center's award-winning programs. Fifteen years later this board continues to advise on programmatic and curricular development. The staff's commitment to partnership with, and responsiveness to, teacher and school needs contributes to the center's success as one of the most heavily attended museum education programs in the state, if not New England.

That should do the trick.

If your staff is not qualified for some aspects of the work, do you have a plan to help them acquire those skills, or to collaborate with and learn from others who do? Faced with important work and no in-town archivist, the Carlisle Historical Society hired a consulting archivist to provide training for society volunteers and town employees while she assessed and organized the two collections. The grant-funded work made the society competitive for a scholar-in-residence grant from a collaboration of state funders, and for another award from the local cultural council for a photo identification project by mother-daughter volunteers. Each time the funder was assured of professional quality because a qualified consultant supervised and trained volunteers while contributing to the completion of significant projects.

How long have your leaders been in place? Some foundations, probably many, are reluctant to fund an organization in the first year of the new director's appointment unless the organization or program is well known to them. The funder may be concerned that the project will not be continued past this award, and therefore any gift now would have less impact than another grant later on in the new tenure. To attract funding during the new director's honeymoon period, the project must be critical to core activities and have its own track record. For the staff already in place, what is the retention rate? A high degree of staff turnover is a danger sign to the reader. If this is your situation, be able to explain it and describe how you are compensating.

Do not overlook the importance of volunteers in demonstrating your institutional worthiness. That you have them shows a connection to the community. That they do important things for you demonstrates their support of your mission and priorities. Be able to show a healthy volunteer program doing meaningful work in appropriately defined jobs with supervision, training, and rewards, as well as the use of management policies mirroring your personnel policies for screening, hiring, and firing. (Be sure your insurance liability policies include the volunteers.) Your volunteer cadre is an excellent source for testimonials and community feedback, new ideas, networking, and fund-raising. Their experiences outside your museum are an important communication tool—they spread the word about the museum and they share the local buzz with you. The donor knows a strong volunteer program is a good indication of a strong institution. Capitalize on this and show off your volunteers.

PLANNING

Can you provide evidence of planning? Is there a rationale for your choice of planning tools and how you use them? For museums this means an interpretive plan and a collections plan. Cultural resource and open-space protection agencies will have master plans and preservation plans. All should have strategic plans. Be able to explain how these plans were developed. Do you use them to set goals and monitor progress? Explain how the proposal supports the appropriate plan. If you don't have these plans, your regional museum association can probably provide examples and point you to others who have successfully developed plans and may be willing to advise you or recommend good consultants to help you.

Strategic Planning

In 2002 the Institute of Museum and Library Services changed its General Operating Support application to a Learning Opportunities Grant and in the process tied much of the application to how the proposed project fulfills the goals of the institution's strategic plan. Reviewers will not tolerate a breezy answer but must have real evidence that you researched and planned before you submitted your proposal.

The Webb-Deane-Stevens Museum in Wethersfield, Connecticut, has a powerful plan they can use to justify their projects and programs.[8] Grants from the Hartford Fund for Public Giving, a community foundation, funded a consultant in 1999 who conducted an organizational assessment, and Laura Roberts, a management consultant to cultural nonprofits, who worked with the museum to develop the strategic plan in 2001. It's a fine example of a funder from the neighborhood helping an organization strengthen itself. Having the plan strengthened the museum's successful proposal to IMLS through its Learning Opportunities Grant to fund "Silas Deane Online." Here are some of the reviewers' positive responses to the proposal's relationship with the strategic plan:

> Explained the institution's needs relative to the use of technology to increase its audience. Right from the start, explained this need as a direct outcome from the Strategic Plan . . . Professional Strategic Plan which touched on all aspects of the museum operation. The plan included financial components as well as implementation strategies. . . . The project proposed is a natural progression of the mission of the museum and an enhancement of a program already in place.

> Very good presentation of museum's strategic plan and how project connects with your efforts to expand audiences. . . . Project is excellent fit for museum's overall strategic plan and fulfills organization's mission to a high degree.

> Involvement from the Board of Managers and staff is stated in Strategic Plan summary. . . . the Strategic Plan identified Ac-

tion steps relating specifically to the educational programs and the importance of basing new programs on collections support.

It's worth noting that the museum's 2001 plan includes fundraising work within its goals. It divides the work into three parts: "donations from individuals, grants from public and private institutional funders, and earned income including Museum fundraisers." The plan begins with "family" cultivation and spreads to field funders such as the Connecticut Humanities Council and NEH and then moves to the outer ring of private foundations beyond Connecticut. This plan doesn't just assign funder names to future projects, it begins by cultivating relationships with funders.

Financial Planning

Sally Zinno points out that many museums have multiyear strategic plans for programs, facilities, and operations, but often the plan is not accompanied by a multiyear budget that indicates what the plan will cost to implement. A museum that develops budgets beyond the current fiscal year can identify trouble and take corrective action. A realistic multiyear budget considers the economic condition of the community and funders, and the museum's own financial experience.

The Ford Foundation report identified financial planning as a common area of weakness. Financial strength is an obvious interest to a cash donor, so cash flow trouble and debt-reduction requests are danger signs. The "dubious funding breakthroughs" mentioned in "When Projects Flounder" would certainly include income projections based on untested fund-raising programs or unrealistic expectations for attendance income for a new building. Here are examples of careful financial predictions winning the day.

- When Historic Georgetown, Inc., a preservation society in Colorado, made projections for its proposed Gateway Visitors Center, HGI was able to show current and expected rates of use and therefore income. Faithful records for the temporary center combined with the state's traffic information for Interstate 70's Eisenhower Tunnel were the basis. Counting only one rider, not the potential four or more, of a portion of the cars using the tunnel, stopping in Georgetown, and spending less than $2.00 each on food, souvenirs, and travel necessities produced an honest and positive operating balance and convinced the funders.
- The Sandwich Glass Museum's income projections for the new museum and working glass furnace included *no new income* but covered increased expenses through operational savings of a new septic system replacing the current need for monthly pumping.

For both Historic Georgetown, Inc., and Sandwich Glass Museum, responsible budget projections reassured donors of a safe investment.

Thematic Planning

Any funder will also look for evidence of planning unique to your field and institution. The list is long—plans for collections, interpretation, furnishing, education, conservation and preservation, exhibits, visitor studies, institutional evaluation, and fundraising. The plan's role is to focus the institution's thoughts on an area of work, identify strengths and weaknesses, develop priorities, assign responsibility and resources, set and measure goals, and connect the work to the institution's strategic plan.

There is no shelf life for any of these plans. They go out of date upon completion. You must show that you review these plans at least annually; more frequent reviews are desirable. Can you demonstrate how those reviews have caused you to change or reaffirm your work, and that those changes are reflected in the renewed plan? Show that you use your field's planning tools to your best advantage.

PROFESSIONAL STANDARDS AND BEST PRACTICE

It is not the funder's responsibility to understand your field's standards. As with planning, identify those most appropriate to your work and demonstrate that you have either achieved them or are in a planned process to achieve them. Participation in AAM's MAP (Museum Assessment Program) is a clear indication of just that. The program is appropriate for most organizations when they are ready to commit to self-study. It has assessment modules for institutional administration, collections management, public dimension, and governance.

AAM accreditation is another tool for demonstrating adherence to field standards. For many funders, accreditation "provides credible evidence that the museum not only fulfills its purpose and attains the goals that it proclaims in its mission, but does so in accordance with the highest professional standards." Accreditation is not a prerequisite for funding, but a funder would find that the characteristics of an accredited museum and a fundable institution are related. Do not consider accreditation for funding's sake, but do explore its appropriateness for improving or maximizing your institution's performance. It may be a process that will strengthen your position in the grant game.

Certainly AAM accreditation is not appropriate for all sites; other forms of field recognition may be more achievable. As a historic property, perhaps you can point to the endorsement of National Register listing or National Landmark Status. Blithewold, Historic Georgetown, and the Bell County Historical Society (Minnesota) can all say that one or more of their buildings is a National Register Site. The Paul Revere House is a National Historic Landmark. If you cannot claim pinnacles of industry standards, you should be able to explain why you have not attempted this, when you will, or what prevents you from qualifying.

What are codes of behavior for your organization? There are written ethical standards for boards, volunteers and volunteer managers, conservators, members of AASLH and AAM, and probably many others. Be sure you know which apply to your work and that all the people in your work adhere to them. Preparing your own institution's statement is important, too. Attention to board and staff personal collecting is important in any collecting institution. Attending to investments without conflicts of interest is critical also. Your institution may go a step further by choosing not to invest in some businesses because they conflict with the institution's mission or sensibilities; you may choose not to host certain exhibits because of their tone or because some of the objects are inappropriate. The key is to identify the appropriate codes of behavior and performance and follow them.

ARE YOU A GOOD PARTNER FOR A FOUNDATION?

The foundation will need to feel comfortable with the institution as a partner in both appearance and effect. The foundation officers ask themselves: Does this organization do something we believe in, in a way we can endorse? Does it behave in a way that encourages us to be associated with it?

Mission Match

Your mission and the donor's mission must intersect at the core of both sets of priorities, not on the margins of either. Be sure there is a mission match by talking to the foundation staff early on. A mission statement says what you do, for whom, how you do it, and why it is important.

You can expect your target foundation to have a mission statement, too. Read it carefully and with caution.

There are two barriers to correctly reading and assessing the foundation's mission: being overly optimistic and misjudging thresholds. "Close enough" is too optimistic and not an acceptable match criterion. Your best clues are that some of the language matches exactly. If it's close, don't hesitate to point out that you "believe our goal of adaptive restoration of downtown structures matches your commitment to revitalizing the community while respecting the built environment." Or "by providing after-school clubs in biology, technology, and history, the Museum of Natural History's After-School Clubs Program fulfills the XYZ foundation's commitment to providing safe and dependable opportunities for educational enrichment for inner-city youth during weekday out-of-school-hours."

If your match is not as tight as these, then look into the project's rank in the giving priority. Is your core theme one of their priorities? Does historic preservation appear first in the list or as an afterthought? Is education in the school a higher priority than education for a visiting public? Are cultural resources first or last on the list? Mutual interests in reenactments or historical publications are easy to spot. For other projects like education pro-

WHY ARE YOU THE ONE?

grams, teacher training, or exhibits, be sure that the alignment follows through to the subject matter, audience, and process. Your topical ideas for an exhibit on the Underground Railroad may mesh with those of the donor, but if your audience is students in comfortable suburban schools and the donor targets underserved audiences, your missions do not match. A donor interested in history education may abhor technology and online delivery. Check out recent grants and see what proportion over recent cycles has gone to your priority area.

Thresholds come into play when you stretch the geographic area, audience, subject, participants' age range, or the delivery methods; basically, whenever you stretch the relationship between your project and their mission, you are crossing a threshold of tolerance in the funder. The threshold for "maybe, if we have enough funds" is very low and not the one you want to be in. If you have a twist or innovation to offer, it can't draw your program off-mission. If your project doesn't match their priorities, then no matter how well you prepare your proposal, it will be at a disadvantage.

Sometimes the foundation's interests and mission are so broad that most projects will "fit." This may be a sign of its interest in a real variety of funding opportunities, but assume the statement is not as well focused as their intent, and then call to confirm the match. Fulfilling expectations may not be enough for the donor. In your conversation, you will quickly learn whether they expect you to offer new solutions or alert them to new issues in your proposal.

Do You Behave Well?

Do you exhibit behaviors and values the funder wants to be associated with? A good partner, from the foundation's external point of view, is credible, applies its mission internally and externally, provides good public associations and positioning, and will strengthen the donor's reputation. The Prince Charitable Trusts' support of Blithewold Mansion, Gardens, and Arboretum in Bristol, Rhode Island, is an example of a donor's commitment to an institution as much because of its intrinsic qualities and the behavior of the historic property's staff, volunteers, and supporters as for its management promise and proof of quality.

In Public

If you are a preservation organization, show how the organization, you, your staff, and volunteers support the cause in and out of work. Do you and they participate on the historical commission, maintaining a scenic streetscape or landscape, preserving other buildings to use as offices or an education center? If the director owns and is restoring her own home, find a way to mention that as an extension of your preservation ethos. Basically, the funder is wondering if you behave well on your own terms.

Do you behave well in your community? Do you encourage collaboration, participate in free admission days, sit on community boards, or have a charitable edge? Can you show an understanding of your environment and your donors'?

If the community foundation is addressing homelessness and you collaborate with the housing authority, the public schools, and the local historic houses to offer a four-month program on Saturdays that offers child care and out-of-hours programming on history and historic homes, while parents are in home ownership training, a tax credit–based rehabilitation program, or working with Habitat for Humanity to build their next house on a reclaimed site, you're demonstrating excellent partner behavior while fulfilling your mission and helping all your collaborators and funders fulfill theirs.

In Private

Internally, are you reasonable, if not terrific, to work with? From the foundation's point of view a good partner says "thank you," manages the program honestly and in communication with the funder, and reports honestly and promptly.

Designate a single person as the main contact between your two organizations. Provide useful, but not burdensome, updates and meet all donor inquiries happily. Again, note from the outset the donor's reporting requirements so that as you proceed with the project you can gather the correct information in the appropriate manner. If you encounter difficulties in any part of the project, keep the donor informed. The donor staff's considerable experience may be the perspective you need to help you solve your problem. In cases of real trouble, the donor may wish to become more involved with the project to ensure its success, so do not assume a donor will abandon you if all does not proceed according to plan.

If you see opportunities to support or promote the donor, contact the staff to see whether it is appropriate. If you are asked for a radio interview, check to see whether you can and should mention the donor on the air. If some of the students' work is particularly appealing, get permission to send the donor a copy for use in the annual report, display in their offices, or just to say thank you. If a publication or project they funded wins an award, be sure the donor knows and receives a copy of the award letter.

CONCLUSION

When you apply for a grant, you are asking the funder to make an investment in your organization. Such a commitment requires due diligence on both sides of the check. By demonstrating your worthiness for this investment, you simplify the diligence process for the foundation and demonstrate your knowledge of proper responsibilities and behavior associated with the trust they are being asked to bestow. There is no substitute. Perhaps because we know in our own souls that we are doing our very best and that a little help can make all the difference, we grow impatient with explaining the situation yet again. That is understandable, but irrelevant. What you cannot afford through earned income, you must earn through grants. You earn grant income by developing and cultivating productive relationships with funders by understanding their needs, interests, and expectations; providing excellent and/or innovative programming to address shared missions; preparing useful and readable proposals; and managing funded projects well.

Now let's examine fundable projects more closely.

NOTES

1. Ken Ristine of the Ben B. Cheney Foundation gets full credit for articulating this important step in the process.

2. W. K. Kellogg Foundation, "Building an Organization to Last: Reflections and Lessons Learned from SeaChange" (July 2003), 5.

3. Hope Alswang, then at the New York State Council for the Arts and Advisory Council member, Concord Museum, Massachusetts.

4. I thank Laura Roberts, management consultant to cultural nonprofits, for her comments on the importance of recognizing the values of excellence and innovation as often separate goals.

5. Grant Craft, "When Projects Flounder" (New York: Ford Foundation, 2003), 3–4.

6. The entire section on assessing financial stability was provided by Sally Zinno, management and financial consultant to arts and cultural organizations.

WHY ARE YOU THE ONE?

7. W. K. Kellogg Foundation, "Building an Organization to Last, at www.wkkf.org/Pubs/PhilVol/SeaChange1_00251_03771.pdf.

8. Prepared by Laura Roberts, management consultant to cultural nonprofits.

Case: Commitment and Ability: The Prince Charitable Trusts and Save Blithewold, Inc.

Blithewold Mansion

BLITHEWOLD'S SITUATION

Blithewold is a thirty-three-acre country garden estate begun in the 1890s by Augustus and Bessie Van Wickle as their summer retreat. Bessie Van Wickle was a very accomplished horticulturist and her greatest wish was to have enough good land to establish gardens and an arboretum. Daughter Marjorie inherited her mother's talents, and Bessie and Marjorie spent the rest of their lives developing this beautiful property on Narragansett Bay.

A carriage house, a summerhouse, cottages, a garage, greenhouses, saltwater and freshwater pump houses, and a boathouse and dock on the bay complement the family's turn-of-the-century, forty-five-room English country manor. The landscape

View from Narragansett Bay, Blithewold Mansion, Gardens & Arboretum, Bristol, Rhode Island. Blithewold is an early twentieth-century summer estate now open to the public as a 33-acre cultural landscape. It is listed on the National Register of Historic Places. Courtesy of Save Blithewold, Inc. Photography by Jan Douglas Armor.

is a lush collection of two thousand trees and shrubs represent-
ing three hundred species, both native and exotic, with two miles
of walks through a dozen different gardens and environments,
from the Bamboo Grove to the Oriental Water Garden to the Gi-
ant Sequoia—the tallest specimen on the East Coast. Blithewold's legacy as an intact garden estate makes it an important
destination for horticulturists and historic landscape enthusiasts.

Twenty-five years after Marjorie bequeathed this historic
home and grounds and a significant endowment to a nonprofit organization, serious financial problems threatened the property. In
1999, years of deficit operations forced the layoffs of nearly all
full-time Blithewold staff and greatly reduced the number of public programs. Worse, the leaders began to seriously consider a
proposal to lease the property to a developer—perhaps restricting
or prohibiting public access for the future. Worried supporters
formed Save Blithewold, Inc., and in just six weeks raised
$650,000 in emergency gifts and pledges to acquire a ninety-
nine-year lease from the trust and provide partial operating support. Save Blithewold, Inc., obtained its 501(c)(3) status in 2000.

Save Blithewold, Inc., adopted a revised mission statement in
2003 as part of a yearlong strategic planning process: "To preserve New England's finest garden estate through excellence in
horticulture and historic preservation, and by our example to
teach and inspire others." Blithewold offers classes, lectures, and
tours for preservationists, enthusiasts, serious horticulturists,
and novice gardeners of all ages across Rhode Island. The gardens are open all year and the mansion is open seasonally for
self-guided tours from April through mid-October and in De-
cember. Special events and tours draw thirty thousand visitors
annually for music and theatrical programs from classical con-
certs in the winter to outdoor performances in the summer.

At present the board is engaged in a capital campaign to create an endowment and fund the combined restoration and reconstruction of its grand Lord and Burnham glasshouse. In the 1930s much of the complex was dismantled when heating became too expensive. It once included a rose house, plant house, and the Palm House, but today what survives is the greenhouse with its head house (for equipment and systems controls) and propagating house. With restoration, the complex will have water and heat efficiently managed through new automatic systems as well as the space to propagate plants for the present and future of Blithewold's gardens. Visitors will be able to explore a fully operational estate greenhouse, restored to its original style and use. The restoration will dramatically increase the variety and number of programs offered and will significantly enhance the organization's ability to sustain its important plantings into the next century. The Prince Charitable Trusts' gifts between 1999 and 2003 supported immediate protection of the site from public sale and provided operating support for an interpretive horticulturist and contributions to the endowment.

THE PRINCE CHARITABLE TRUSTS

The Prince Charitable Trusts make about $2.5 million in grants in Rhode Island each year, recently almost exclusively on Aquidneck Island or for programs that affect the quality of life on the island. Kristin Pauly, managing director of the trusts' Washington, D.C., office, and codirector of the Rhode Island grant program, says that "When Blithewold was in serious financial trouble . . . the dedication of the staff . . . brought the problem to the attention of several community leaders in the area of historic preservation and horticulture. . . . Mrs. Frederick Prince was alerted to the 'Save Blithewold' effort and she was inspired by the unique historic value of the property and the gardens to suggest that the trusts make a contribution to the effort to re-structure the ownership and operation of Blithewold." Pauly visited the site and discussed the plans for the new management structure. When the trusts made a significant grant that year, the compelling conditions were "the dedication of the staff in trying to save the house and gardens, and the network of patrons in that part of the state who were willing to step forward in response to the dire situation."

In this case, Blithewold's mansion, gardens, and arboretum did some of the work themselves. Clearly they had inspired staff, volunteers, and supporters to work for a better solution. The site had the same effect on Pauly and the Prince family: "There is a unique sense of history and the site has an unusual beauty." Pauly believes that this intrinsic value will continue "to influence the organization's destiny." That is not enough reason for initial or continued support, of course, but it was a good opening sequence.

During her continued visits and attendance at events Pauly saw encouraging signs. She believes

> the major breakthrough for ... Blithewold ... was hiring Eric Hertfelder to be the executive director. He ... brought excellent management to the operation. This ... added to the garden expertise in the existing (and new) staff, creates a wonderful combination. He has been creative about broadening the base of support for the organization and in understanding the full range of possibilities for income and support. In addition, he seems to have been able to draw the best from the existing staff and volunteers, while hiring new staff with good qualifications. There is a dedicated group of volunteers—at both the level of direct participation and in leadership.

The Trusts have made three gifts to Blithewold, the most recent as a final, three-year grant that it believes will contribute to stabilizing the organization and positioning it to find ongoing sources of support. Pauly and the Prince family were prepared to invest in Blithewold because its staff, volunteers, and supporters inspired partnership in a project compelling to the people in both organizations, and because the people at Blithewold were able to aspire to and perform the functions necessary to sustain an organization beyond the initial rescue operation.

Visitor Center at Historic Georgetown, Inc.

Case: Partnership and Planning: Historic Georgetown, Inc.

In this mountain town of 950 people, on the interstate connection between Denver and the Rocky Mountain ski slopes, a small historic preservation organization has steadily protected landscapes, structures, and the history of this mining community for its role in the development of the American West. Georgetown, Colorado, was designated a National Historic Landmark District in 1966. Its history as the first silver mining town in the state has taken Georgetown from camp to boom to bust like so many others. The period of near-ghost-town status was its saving grace, leaving enough structures intact—from fire towers and boardwalks to miners' cabins and owners' mansions—for a "well-rounded view of the lifestyles of a Victorian-era mining town." For over thirty-one years, Historic Georgetown, Inc. (HGI), has purchased, restored, and interpreted five residential sites depicting

Visitor Center, Historic Georgetown, Inc., Georgetown, Colorado. Courtesy of Pixel Ditties, Denver, Colorado.

the daily life of the range of Georgetown residents during the silver mining decades from the 1850s through the 1890s.

HGI's early partnerships with the county commissioners and the town of Georgetown led it to alliances with the Colorado Division of Housing, the Colorado State Historical Fund, the Colorado Historical Society, and the Colorado Department of Transportation, all for historic preservation projects. Historic Georgetown, Inc., has won awards from the National Trust for Historic Preservation, the American Association for State and Local History, and the Colorado Historical Society for its preservation excellence. It has effectively managed more than $3.5 million in government, foundation, and corporate grants and private gifts over that time. HGI is an excellent partner. Two projects, the Mahany Building and the Gateway Visitors Center, demonstrate HGI's successful partnership strategy.

The Mahany Building, sadly and affectionately known as BOB, the Burnt-Out Building, had stood derelict on Taos at 6th Street since 1974. HGI rescued the building, refurbishing the interior into two low-income housing units and one commercial space. In its winter 2001–2002 newsletter, HGI staff wrote: "HGI was able to undertake this project thanks to a number of donors who believed in one of the underlying principles of historic preservation: that seemingly impossible projects can be successfully completed with the creation of innovative and meaningful partnerships." The $350,000 project restored a historic structure, created affordable housing and business space to contribute to the local economy, and improved the condition of the neighborhood. This triple achievement attracted funds and advice from the town of Georgetown, Clear Creek County Commissioners, the Xcel Foundation of Denver, Clear Creek National Bank, Clear Creek Economic Development Corporation, and the Colorado Division of Housing. The project won a 2002

Steven Hart Award from the Colorado Historical Society. It also came in under budget. At the award ceremony, Barbara S. Hornby, then president of the Colorado Historical Society, spoke proudly of HGI's work overall: "As Williamsburg dramatizes the founding propositions of seventeenth- and eighteenth-century America, as Mystic is to the whaling industry, so Georgetown and Silver Plume without rival can tell the story of the American West in the nineteenth century." The partnership worked so well that even after the goals were achieved, it kept working for HGI by triggering an invaluable third-party endorsement.

The Gateway Visitor Center project demonstrated how planning care and partnerships with other groups would convince funders that your organization is a worthwhile investment. They planned the project to develop in three phases over six years. It involved purchasing property, operating a temporary center, achieving official designations and endorsements, plus fundraising and construction. Each step required enormous amounts of time, patience, and thoroughness. Earning across-the-board acceptance was key. Foremost was designation by the Colorado Department of Transportation as an official rest site in the highway system. Then came earning plan endorsements from the town and county governments, the state's Division of Wildlife and Department of Highways, the Historical Society, the county tourism board, the town of Silver Plume, and local residents and merchants. Projections based on use at the temporary visitors center and from related facilities such as the Eisenhower Tunnel on I-70 convinced observers of the real need and the financial viability. HGI was the one organization that could pull together a project that interested all the participants. HGI's investment of time, energy, and good planning convinced all the other players to invest as well.

Why Project Money Will Be Your First Money

Today's fierce funding competition means there are fewer differences between a fundable *project* and a fundable *organization*. Still, your first grant from any funder will probably be for a project rather than for general support. The Westborough Historical Commission's Nathan Fisher House case with this chapter is an example of a first-time project application that has all the necessary components.

Project money is a good starter grant because there is less risk to a funder endorsing a carefully described *program* with a beginning, middle, and end, and specific goals and project outlays, than to a funder endorsing an entire *organization*. To make the decision to fund a project, the funder must learn enough about the organization to have faith in it, but will not delve as deeply into board, staff, and financial policies and functions for a $5,000 grant for wallpaper in the parlor as it would for a $50,000 endowment contribution.

A fundable project has the qualities of a fundable organization, but on a smaller scale:

- Support of mutual missions
- Demonstrable need
- An identifiable and appropriate audience
- Uniqueness and quality
- Sensible budget, resources, and planning

Let's drill down to the components you need to make your case. You'll recognize them all, but perhaps these examples will simplify your preparation.

MISSION MATCH

As always, your mission and the donor's must match and the project's goals must support both missions. If the project doesn't support the donor's mission, they won't read the proposal. If the donor cannot tell how the project supports your mission, they won't fund it. The funder will want to be sure that the money isn't spent on a project that is just useful; they want to fund one best suited to help the organization succeed. A fascinating project with strong funding possibilities can tempt any of us to consider crossing our mission's boundary. Mission creep is a real danger for innovative and hungry organizations. Constantly rechecking the project's support of your mission keeps your compass calibrated.

ORGANIZATIONAL NEED

Usually, the audience's needs will trump institutional needs as a funder's motivation. Still, when a project builds the organization's capacity to do its work well, that is when your own needs will attract a donor interested in the institution, either as a method of reaching the intended audience or of doing the special-interest work it values. Describe the project as a solution and/or opportunity. When the state department of education changes curriculum guidelines to mandate third-grade local history study and the teachers have never taught this before, the need is for content and training (to solve the problem) and encouraging teachers' continued use of your services (an income opportunity).

When rain comes in through the ell's roof, and you have had to take another entire room off the tour because you need it to safely store the objects from the ell, the needs are to fix the roof, protect the collection, and return the dining hall to public access. You now have options in approaching funders. Where one will respond to the conservation issues of sealing the building envelope, another will be interested in providing public access to the historic room. Another funder might want to support the opportunity to conduct a proper inventory during the move and rehouse the objects after you fix the roof. Who is this roof project for—the house, the visitors, and/or the objects? Be sure you can describe them adequately in number, size, characteristics, uniqueness, and impact. Is the roof an original in need of special care, or a poor substitute requiring appropriate replacement? Why are the sixteen linear feet of photograph albums and scrapbooks important to your interpretation? Why are they important to the donor? Be able to describe what the project means in terms of public access, a contribution to the historic community, or both together.

AUDIENCE NEED

The only difference between describing the audience's need for a project and for operating support is scale. You have a smaller target audience and, hopefully, highly specific information for describing them and making your case. If your guests are maritime history aficionados and you are the best example of a nineteenth-century shipowner's home, you can easily explain that having the counting house off-limits because the roof leaks would interfere with your work and disappoint your visitors. If your target audience is students in the rural mountain towns, you can make an excellent case for the need to fund staff visits, loan boxes, and loan displays for them instead.

UNIQUENESS

Funders have a real and justifiable concern about redundancy in nonprofit work: too many groups doing the same thing without the efficiencies of scale. Explain away their worries by identifying competing programs, service gaps, or novel opportunities that illustrate why your plan is appropriate. Developing income-generating birthday parties may not be unique, but the content may be. The specialty you're offering is industrial archaeology research for exhibits, teacher support units, *and* the self-sustaining birthday-party archeology "digs."

QUALITY

There are many, many evaluation tools available, but don't let the evaluation specter overwhelm you. Whichever one you choose, make sure it's the most appropriate tool for the project at hand, not just a well-known tool. First, see what the donor requires. Use existing evaluation tools whenever possible to accrue data comparable over time and to reduce the design burden, but if you need a new tool to fit your situation, ask your colleagues what they use. If any proves better than the donor's recommended tool, ask the donor about substituting the more appropriate one, or combining the two in order to serve your purposes and theirs.

The donor may not realize that good exhibit planning includes beginning, middle (including mock-ups), and end evaluation. So explain it. *Front-end evaluation* identifies public interest in, understanding of, and response to, concepts, themes, and formats. In *formative evaluation* you pilot the program or mock-up an exhibit to test public response to your ideas. IMLS encourages "rapid prototyping"—in a short period during the development process, you prepare a test example and ask a preselected focus group to comment on its success. The *summative* or *remedial evaluation* comes after the program is in place or the exhibit is open.

Remember, you don't just evaluate for the donor, but so that you can improve your work.

BUDGET, RESOURCES, AND SUSTAINABILITY

These three topics of budget, resources, and sustainability often appear together on an application form because they are interconnected. They all influence your ability to carry out your proposed project.

Budget

Whether you are applying to NEH, a regional funder, or the local corporate leader, you must present a good business approach with numbers and accountability. Budgets must show the cost of the project and the sources of funds for that work. Listing just the expense side will not do. PR and marketing consultant Dorothy Chen-Courtin cautions organizations to make financial projections based on historical data—and be faithful to them. Don't lead the data where you want to go. Be realistic about growth potential for the institution and its programs, because your success will be judged by your real numbers compared to predictions.

Do not cheat yourself on overheads, utilities, and staff time in particular. Break out what percentage of staff time is involved and the corresponding percentage of salary and benefits that should be applied directly to the project. Locate real numbers on health, dental, and disability insurance; FICA, unemployment, and retirement costs; and worker's compensation. If you're managing a collaborative project, don't be shy about including 5 to 10 percent of the project cost as a line item that addresses director's oversight, financial management, and good old heat and light.

Keep the budget simple and readable—if it's too vague, the financial whizzes will be uncomfortable; if it's too complicated the nonfinancial types will give up. To make sure you don't leave out important costs, a little mental rehearsal will help. Walk through the whole project in your head—as the event manager and as the visitor. Have you included costs for planning time and materials; promotion; site use and any extras such as rented coat racks, valet parking, and extra parking space, a policeman, and lighting or heat or fans for rented tents? Are there extra costs for adjunct staff, transportation, or a hotel room because the flights are at inconvenient times? If you have to convert some to in-kind contributions, fine; just be sure you demonstrate that you know what the project really costs. Funders will always see the gaps in your budget and wonder if you are really prepared to pull this off without paying for the speaker to actually travel to your state.

WHY PROJECT MONEY WILL BE YOUR FIRST MONEY

Staff and Other Resources

Remember to let the donor know who at your organization is actually doing this work. It shows that you've thought carefully about delivery, and that you've identified the skills appropriate for successfully completing it. If that means bringing in staff, fine; if you have the right staff already, that might be one reason why you are best suited for this project.

A resource is not always cash, but it always means something valuable in cash terms. Resources can be staff and volunteer time, copying and program supplies, meeting rooms, exhibits, or buses to be used. When you have a board member loath to help with asking for money, perhaps he or she can help locate other resources. Free use of a row of shelves in the town hall's safe, contributed design services, or access to the parent organization's photography equipment, scanner, and computer are all resources supporting your work. The logs for building the Job Carr Cabin Museum were an in-kind contribution. What a difference that made! Identify these contributions so the funder knows you know what you need and to show there are other sources of support for the project.

Sustainability

The sustainability discussion is a minefield: If you can sustain the program, why do you need this grant? If you have other funders in mind, why ask this one? If you don't have any, how can you explain how you'll fund it without them in the future? Your only approach is to explain the situation fully by answering each of these questions before they come up. You can address these questions from a position of strength *if* you develop a three-year funding plan tied to your strategic plan—it's harder if you're making it up as you go along. Explain why you're approaching other funders in another cycle, but not now. Perhaps you're completing another project funded by that donor, or you have been invited to a meeting with a funder, but the timing prevents a request and response before the project date during the spring school holidays next year. You may have plans for developing related income-producing projects. Your program for children in Head Start may have another life as a deliverable through area parents' groups; or if the pilot program works, this will become a regular module of your popular summer camps.

There's another piece to the definition of sustainability: continued implementation. If you have a one-time project such as purchasing software or preparing teacher packets, how do you convince the funder that you will continue to use those to their fullest extent? Those teacher packets don't mail themselves. Describe how teachers can request them and who is responsible for sending out the packets, keeping a ready supply, and evaluating their use by adaptation for additional programs or redesigning, where appropriate, for this one. Explain how installing the software, loading the data, and updating the data for the collections software will not be a haphazard affair, but a regular duty of the curatorial assistant that is included in his or her annual work goals with specific targets and expectations. Convince the funder that the project has a continuing role in the life of the organization, life that will be sustained through relevance to continuing work by allocations of staff time and inclusion in performance expectations.

MINDFUL PLANNING—TIME AND TOPIC

How many times have you been told, "It's all in the preparation"? Well, it is. Planning mistakes make for a quick death in a competitive process. Just as for evaluation, there is no shortage of helpful tools out there. Of course, we can each plan without them, but often their detailed suggestions can help you do a more thorough planning job. This is particularly helpful when you're starting an entirely new kind of project or you need to reinvigorate an old one. The IMLS's online "National Leadership Grant Project Planning: A Tutorial" thoroughly explains steps for newcomers: developing scope, identifying the gap between current conditions and your planned result, and targeting and identifying beneficiaries. There is even a mini-lesson on outcomes and outputs for evaluation.

Sumption and Wyland's feasibility analysis tool in table 6.1 covers the qualifying characteristics of a fundable project with an important addition: The executive director and the board must comment on their conclusions.[1] This written summary is extremely valuable when, in the fullness of time, you need to retrace your decision-making process or if new members of the staff or board need to hear why such and such a project was put forward for funding or not.

Time

The trouble with time is that it's elastic only until it runs out. Create a thoughtful timeline that expects the unexpected. Lay it out on paper using the calendar with all your other commitments. Start the timetable with the donor's notification date plus a few weeks, at least. Compensate for inevitable delays in acquiring special supplies such as matching mortars or salvaged timbers for your construction project. Remember to allow for down time during holiday periods for staff, advisors, and participants. Don't forget to include evaluation in the timeline. Leaving it out would be a real problem if you plan to fine-tune the project after the launch.

Table 6.1.   Sumption and Wyland's Project Development Checklist

Prospective Program/Service/Project/Activity
Feasibility Analysis

*(Complete the following analysis by assigning points for the rationale
given in each review area. For example, a program with a clear
funding stream would receive 10 points. A program with no plan for
funding would receive 0 points.)*

Target Area: _____

Service Description:_____

Description of the Target Audience and Geographic Boundaries:

Description of the Proposed Service:

(A)_____ (0 - 20 points) Describe how this program/project enhances the mission of the
Organization.

(B)_____ (0 - 15 points) Describe the methods this program/activity uses to meet a unique
need of a population left unserved without supports.

(C)_____ (0 - 20 points) Describe the projected funding/revenue stream for the proposed
program/service/project. Describe the length and stability of the
funding availability. If funded by soft (grant) funding, describe
the likelihood of ongoing funding to sustain program efforts.

Table 6.1. *(continued)*

(D)_____ (0 - 10 points)   Provide a thorough description of the staffing and administrative needs to support this planned effort.

(E)_____(0 - 10 points)   Provide a thorough description of the facility, equipment, resource, technology, and related support needs of the project at start-up and ongoing.

(F)_____(0 - 10 points)   Describe the liability and exposure of the project to the Agency, its staff, and board.

(G)_____(0 - 10 points)   Describe the methods that will be used to evaluate the success/ outcomes of this project.

Review Criteria

(A)   **Mission**   _____
(B)   **Methods**   _____
(C)   **Funding**   _____
(D)   **Staffing**   _____
(E)   **Facility**   _____
(F)   **Liability**   _____
(G)   **Evaluation**   _____
Total Points   _____

Recommendation by Executive Director:

Recommendation by Board:

If contingency fees are acceptable in a budget, contingency dates work in a timeline. Use them to calculate the end date of your project. Though it is a much like setting your clock ahead to avoid being late (many of us learn to compensate), train yourself to invoke the contingency date only under crisis conditions: uncooperative weather; unavailability of staff, consultants, or volunteers; and dramatic changes in the institution's environment such as shipping strikes or influenza waves in the school system. If you are forced off the schedule, let the donor know immediately. Explain why, and then how you plan to compensate.

Planning with Your Audience

How has your audience helped you develop the program? Surely, as Carol Schreider, head of education at the Minnesota Historical Society, says, don't just consult yourself when planning something for the public! Schreider recommends including audience representatives in the group advising your program and exhibit development. When you move outside your inner circle, be sure that "outside" is not simply interpreted as academic experts outside the museum. As a profession, we have all fallen into the habit, partially through the rightful encouragement by humanities funders, to include scholars on advisory panels, but we have focused on academics without soliciting enough other perspectives. Schreider reminds us "that such consultants [academics] should be used along with experts in audience research, so that the best scholarship can be applied to exhibits and programs that are attractive and intellectually accessible to the intended audience." At Conner Prairie, *Follow the North Star* (see the second case in this chapter) was developed with the assistance of scholars and a psychologist as well as an advisory committee that was predominantly African American. All had a chance to see the first version of the program be-fore it went public.

This can be tense, but it is still worthwhile. Members of one group involving a twentieth-century historian and veterans of the Korean War found their perspectives at odds over interpretation. The project went over-schedule as the two sides identified dis-agreements and worked toward the common goal of an interpre-tation that would accurately depict the events of the police ac-tion, hold the attention of someone who had never been to war, and placed it in the "correct" historical context on the ground and in politics. The funder was frustrated by the delays but was committed to joining the two voices and seeing the project suc-ceed. It granted the extension and was rewarded with a com-pleted project.

The staff at the Kentucky Historical Society recommended that the volunteers at the Bell County Historical Society create an advisory committee, with an outside chairman, to coordinate preparations for the 250th anniversary of Dr. Thomas Walker's exploration of Kentucky. They enlisted a new volunteer as chair because of his many talents, including his experience as a school superintendent with obvious connections to the school system and its culture. The result was a very popular, award-winning school program. It pays to know your audience.

CONCLUSION

If you've done your job well, you may be in a position to ask for renewed support of this project or new support of another. In making this decision, the foundation staff will ask first those questions that have become so familiar: Was the museum a good partner? Did it do a good job the first time around? Was there a careful accounting of money and effort spent? Is the new project a better project? Did you mention the donor appropriately in press releases and media situations? Did you perhaps give them some good sound bytes, images, numbers, or anecdotes that will make it into their annual report?

Of course, the project must compete with others in the current round, but past returns in this case are strong indicators of future performance. You can begin to cultivate the foundation for future general support once its faith in your organization and your work convinces them you are a worthy investment. Perhaps you can even develop the relationship to the point where the foundation is willing to make grants toward operating costs while they are supporting specific projects. Then you surely have momentum.

NOTE

1. Thanks to Michael Wyland of Sumption and Wyland, South Dakota, for the use of this assessment tool.

C_{ase}: P_{roject} M_{oney} a_s
F_{irst} M_{oney}:
$W_{estborough}$ $H_{istorical}$
$C_{ommission}$ a_{nd} t_{he}
N_{athan} F_{isher} H_{ouse}

The Nathan Fisher House

The Westborough Historical Commission is the town government arm responsible for oversight and basic expenses for the
Nathan Fisher House, a town-owned property. The Friends of
the Nathan Fisher House is the 501(c)(3) organization charged
with its improvements and educational programs. The organizations share two board members, ensuring constant coordination.
They also share a clear commitment to preservation work and
have a solid understanding of the importance of community education as a reason for their existence. Increased public understanding of preservation work and its public advantages is critical

The Nathan Fisher House, ca. 1890. This two-part building started in 1820 as
Fisher's store. He added on very fashionable living quarters after his marriage in
1822. It is located on what was then known as the Worcester Turnpike, close by the
Wesson Tavern in the part of town known originally as Wessonville and the center of
Westborough. During the boon years of turnpike travel, business along the main
thoroughfare from Boston to Worcester made Wessonville a commercial hub. Courtesy of Westborough Historical Commission.

to garnering continued support for future preservation work at the Nathan Fisher House and throughout the town.

Westborough is a New England town-meeting town. At the annual meeting each spring, the town's citizens hear and then vote on the town budget as proposed by the finance committee. The Historical Commission can expect to receive between $5,000 and $10,000 annually to pay its staff, oversee guideline compliance for all buildings in the historic district, and care for any historic properties (graveyards, monuments, parks, paths, and buildings) owned by the town. This is not enough to replace all fifty-eight windows, of various sizes, in the Nathan Fisher House, scrape and paint the shutters, and finish the rehabilitated first-floor interior complete with a stair hall painted by the renowned itinerant painter of the nineteenth century, Rufus Porter.

The Friends had to step in. Since the group had evidence of financial support from the community in the form of gifts from individuals through appeals and at special events and demonstrated by in-kind work by the Boy Scouts who scraped and painted all the shutters, there was enough proof of a "going concern" for the Friends to make their first applications for foundation grant support of discrete portions of the project.

To encourage grants from donors who would be overwhelmed by the full project costs, the commission divided the window project into the four sides of the house. Each became a discrete project. The Friends had already raised enough to finance replacements on one short end of the house. The two foundation applications would focus on the longest side, with the most windows, which fronted the highway. The rest would be "sold" for $650 each to community groups such as Rotary and Girl Scouts.

There was one thing they hadn't planned on. The Westborough Historical Commission had an unknown supporter, a resident and a part of the commuter crowd that passed the Nathan Fisher House daily. When the Friends of the Nathan Fisher House applied to the George F. and Sybil H. Fuller Foundation for a grant, they did not know that a champion on the board would be a deciding factor for their grant. The commuting foundation officer had known that the Friends and the town had been operating and caring for the house for the last ten years and had hoped that something would come of it. He considered the application an opportunity to "be a catalyst to spur donations" to the restoration project. Though the application had to qualify under terms of geographic and programmatic priorities, this officer's role as the project champion helped secure a gift.

Both foundations awarded grants in the amounts requested, totaling $11,000. With that glorious show of support from outside the community, the Friends approached the town at the annual meeting on behalf of the Historical Commission requesting a bold $40,000 for help with the community group's windows plus interior finishes following window installation that would restore the building to town and public use. The Friends warned the town that foundations and corporations no longer gave money for business as usual, but only in support of going concerns with clear community support. The citizenry granted the $40,000 in thanks for outside money earned and in hopes of more to come. Now there would be momentum to attract corporate support from Westborough's growing high-tech corporate residents.

The window project was successful because it

- had a clear, manageable scope
- was achievable based on the organization's history of funding replacement of all the internal systems (plumbing, heating, and electrical)

- served the clear purpose in completing exterior renovations that were delaying interior renovations and therefore full use of the house for the town and citizens
- had an engaged donor at the foundation
- brought with it existing support
- leveraged future support while supporting the missions of the donors and the recipients

That momentum triggered a $50,000 appropriation from the commonwealth to promote the site for pubic and visitor use. It's a good way to make progress.

Case: Partnership, Uniqueness, and Excellence: Conner Prairie and the Nina Mason Pulliam Charitable Trust

Follow the North Star Program

Conner Prairie is a 1,400-acre outdoor living history museum in Fishers, Indiana, less than a half hour's drive from Indianapolis. Its museum center and five historic areas together "serve as a local, regional and national center for education and activities exploring the lives, times and values of the 1800s in America." Conner Prairie is a superpower museum, but like the rest of us, each of its projects must still compete for funding with those from equally powerful institutions: the Indianapolis Children's Museum, the Eiteljorg Museum of American Indians and Western Art, Indiana State Museum, and the Indianapolis Zoo.

Follow the North Star is an immersion program about the Underground Railroad. Participants take on the experience of runaway slaves making their way to safety. Cinda Baldwin, grants

Follow the North Star Program. Participants in Conner Prairie's renowned program, *Follow the North Star,* face uncertainty with every step as fugitive slaves traveling the Underground Railroad. The program runs each April and November. Courtesy of Conner Prairie Shawn Spence Photography.

manager at Conner Prairie, describes the program: "Participants
... step back into history and fill the shoes of fugitive slaves making their way through the Indiana countryside and our historic
buildings. Continually on guard against misfortune and deceit,
hoping to reach freedom, they *Follow the North Star.*"

What makes *Follow the North Star* fundable? It has all the
components of grant readiness:

- meaningful work for a definable audience of mutual interest to the donor and the museum
- a target audience with demonstrable need
- a quality, innovative product with measurable results
- a return on investment for the donor and the museum
- third-party recognition in the form of an AASLH award
  for quality
- thoughtful research, development, and continued management

Conner Prairie (CP) is as an established institution with a
great deal of clout and name recognition, and reams of successful grants in its history. Therefore, making the case for the
institution is not as important as making the case for this project as the best way to fulfill the museum's and the donor's
shared goals.

Follow the North Star had its beginning as part of an institutional effort and the project focus of the application to Nina Mason Pulliam Charitable Trust (NMPCT). Between 1996 and
2002, CP initiated a new interpretive program design to attract
and serve ethnically and racially diverse audiences. Since CP believes its mission is "best accomplished by encouraging active
participation and immersion in programming," the staff focuses
its programmatic efforts on hands-on, spend-the-weekend, and

total immersion programs where visitors become characters in the event or process they are exploring.

CP applied to the NMPCT for a project based on *Follow the North Star:* outreach to the Indianapolis Public Schools with discounted participation in the program. This would be a new audience and a more diverse audience for CP—two of its project goals. It seemed a good match for NMPCT with its intent to serve an audience without access to museum programs and to contribute to the life of the community. In this joint project, the museum and NMPCT could reduce admission fees by 50 percent and cover transportation expenses to overcome the cost barrier for their student audience and provide access to an exceptional learning opportunity.

The figures in table 4.2 show project goals, strategies, and outcomes for the 2001–2002 project. The museum achieved those goals, and NMPCT funded the project for a second year. The museum exceeded its 2003 goals.

Michael Twyman, director of grants programs at NMPCT, says that

> Conner Prairie's *Follow the North Star* provided the Trust a unique opportunity to invest in a quality and significant community program that is both educational and powerful. Not only were we excited to make sure that the local community experienced this worthwhile program but it furthered our objective to [advance] one of our funding priorities: enriching community life. . . .
>
> Our decision to fund the program for a second year was based on the success achieved by Conner Prairie during the first year of our grant relationship. . . . We felt very comfortable with the executive and board leadership at Conner Prairie at the time and saw the *Follow the North Star* program as the most appropriate opportunity by which to partner with an organization to meet our mutual goals.

Twyman has pointed out mutual missions and shared audience; uniqueness, quality, and demonstrable success of the project; confidence in the institution and its leadership; and an interest in partnership in the decision to support CP's project.

Can your potential donors find those qualities in you and your project?

SEVEN

How to Gain Traction

Crossing the threshold to grant readiness is not a noticeable event but an accumulation of circumstances that combines your ability to articulate your value and strengths with evidence of your success in projects or institutional improvements. The case example for this chapter, the Carlisle Historical Society, shows how the convergence of events and the society's responsiveness to opportunity allowed it to gain traction. When you have your house in order and are beginning to apply for grants, you must have evidence to show why you matter, be able to explain what you continue to do to strengthen your situation, and then convince the donor you are a worthy investment.

SHOWING HOW YOU MATTER

You can strengthen future proposals by harnessing basic information that demonstrates your institution's worth. Be ready to broadcast this information for each success. Harnessing your worth is defining your value, and that means collecting information to back up your claims. It starts with good office systems. Tool, or retool, your office to manage collected information that describes what you do, for whom you do it, and why you have chosen to do it. Table 7.1 lists examples of these paper files and appropriate materials for each. If you collect information electronically, keep a computer version of appropriate materials. Use a database to manage contact information; track contacts with the foundation; and record application deadlines, request amounts and dates, and award dates. But it can easily be done with good paper files and a working spreadsheet of current and potential targets.

Keep at least four kinds of numbers available on demand: financial condition, attendance by demographics, marketing research, and evaluation information. Your board should see this regularly, and you should be ready to share it with donors and potential donors whenever the opportunity arises. Financial information should be projected and actual, including figures for attendance, earned income, and gifted income. Be able to provide a summary of the environment or of institutional changes or conditions that affected these numbers. The "as of" information should not be older than a year, and six months is far better.

Documenting Your Work

To help donors visualize and appreciate your work, provide examples by using press and media records, photographs and videos, and evaluation results. This requires the program or project manager to take responsibility for keeping records. Make three copies of any article, press release, photograph, or radio listing—one each for the project, funder, and institutional

Table 7.1.   Building Donor and Grant Files

These files are your backup. They have everything you need for supporting your proposal preparation work.

Field information
Field publications from AASLH and other professional organizations
Third-party reports demonstrating service gaps or programming needs
Newspaper articles and editorials on appropriate community, regional or national issues
Foundation reports on research for your field

Specific support materials: *never send all these support materials with an application, but do have them on hand so that the ones you need are ready when you want them.*
Tax status information—your (501(c)(3) letter
Income and expenses, compared with budget, for year to date
Organization's current operating budget
Most recent annual report, if you create one
Audited financial statements for most recent two years, including any management letters
Board of Directors list
Resumes of key program personnel
Organization chart
List of grants received by organization in most recent years
Awards lists for staff and institution
Accreditation or assessment reports
Strategic plan
Interpretive plan
Exhibition and program schedule

Program or project files
Project or program budget
Images from past programs and from the current one
Anecdotes
List of special attendees or participants
Evaluation results
Final report
Ideas for next time
Potential supporters list

Each funding application file
Funder information sheet including link to on-line annual report if available
Funder history and interests information
Final report for prior grant
Grant application instructions
Copy of the submitted application with all its pristine attachments
Interim updates
Notice letter
Copies of thank you letters and notes from staff, board members and project participants
Reports on all correspondence or communication (e-mail and phone)
Funder's annual report in print if not available on-line

files. Keep those thank you notes from teachers, students, parents, and all other participants. Splurge on color copies of the kids' drawings. Make sure each is annotated with date and source. Your files should also have good quality images—slides, photographs, or digital photographs. Explain to the photographer what kind of photographs will make the strongest case to a funder. These images must show people, activity, color, and the distinctiveness of your institution or project. Be specific about how to record the event (perhaps with the funder's banner or staff in the photo) and how to show high impact (a full audience, a student with a historic character, parents working with kids on a project). Again, make sure each image is annotated with a date, place, and event, and that you have written permissions from the photographer and all the people in the picture to use the images.

Describing Your Audience

Now think about who actually comes to your site or participates in any of your programming. If they will allow it, record your visitors' personal information, either at the cash register, at program registration, or in surveys. If Radio Shack can ask for zip codes, so can you. Describe your audience in categories that make sense to funders. Keep those categories constant across the years for sensible comparisons. It is not just the gate that matters, though. Track visitor numbers in the café and shop, on the Web, and for off-site programs. Please note: If you collect information from website visitors, it is prudent, and may be legally required in your area, to have a privacy policy posted on the site. If you need help creating one, the Direct Marketing Association (www.thedma.org) has a free privacy policy generator on its website that may fit your needs.

HOW TO SHOW YOU ARE A WORTHY INVESTMENT

A worthy investment means a legitimate need. There are two types of need: opportunity and solution. Funders respond to opportunities. Nina Zannieri and the board of the Paul Revere Memorial Association give "a positive cast to expressions of need." Their case is not "'the sky was falling' but rather that we [hope foundations will] see the value in funding a winner, quality programs, value as opposed to need; demand rather than dismay."

You can use success and awards to demonstrate need based on opportunity. When the Sandwich Glass Museum won its Challenge Grant from NEH, it was one of only seven made to historical museums and societies that year. It was clear that if NEH saw an opportunity to support an excellent project, other donors would be excited by the program and by the learning opportunities the new museum would create. You may find that creating a CD on tracing your family history is the new niche for your off-site education efforts. The user's interests and training needs, and the opportunity to safely increase access to your fragile documents while creating a learning resource, is an irresistible combination, and none of it has anything to do with dire straits.

Documenting Need

Whether it's opportunity knocking or problem resolution, you have to document it. Each department can easily keep a phone log of inquiries—the front desk for information, the archives for research help, the development office for membership, the facilities staff for rentals, the café and the shop by receipts. All of these demonstrate your use by your audiences. To be sure the format is appropriate, draft a form for the staff to test, edit, and perfect before asking them to use it regularly. Ask the staff for a weekly report, making it a routine Monday or Friday activity. Keep them all on the same schedule so the numbers relate and you can tell who has not yet submitted information. Remind them, and yourself, that together these weekly records create a picture of your good work—a picture you need to share with others so that you can keep doing good work.

To develop big-picture data for describing your environment, institution, project, and your current and potential users, collect information from city, state, and national sources such as the Department of Education, the Census Bureau, state tourism board, and community websites. Start with the wider environment and then work down to who comes in your door. Is your community on the way up or the way down? What factors of road building, museum building, school building, gentrification, public housing developments, service increases, and so forth affect the life of your community right now and therefore affect what programs you provide, how you work, and your future planning? Describe your competitors and your partners (sometimes they are the same depending upon the project). What are other organizations' visitation rates across the season? What does research from the tourism office tell you about visitors to your area? What does the Department of Education say about the schools' free or reduced meals percentages and the number of students at each school and in each grade? What does the census say for your area about population, economic status, type of industry, language use, ethnicity, and so on?

Here's an example of a case where numbers explain away assumptions of a very wealthy community:

One might assume that a seaside region so close to the Boston Metropolitan area would enjoy access to services and availability of funds. Instead, the Sagamore Bridge over the Cape

Cod Canal separates us from the mainland in unique ways. The Cape (Barnstable County) has a limited corporate base and employment is primarily suburban services and seasonal tourism. Per capita income for Barnstable County is $16,402, 5% below the Commonwealth's average of $17,224. Seventeen percent of the children in our schools qualify for free or reduced lunches—that means income for a family of four of less than $31,000 per year.

These statistics place the Sandwich Glass Museum's request in a community context and clearly demonstrate a need for outside support.

BEGINNING TO USE EVALUATION TOOLS

When you commit to involving evaluation in all you do, be sure to take the time to integrate collecting and using that information into the job expectations of all staff. Extend training to as many as possible, and be prepared to provide the resources of time, money, and support when they follow through. In chapter 3, we discussed the expectations for qualitative and quantitative evaluation becoming so pervasive that no institution can get through a grant application without it. The front-line staff, the educators, and the public relations folks are your best allies in evaluation. Provide training, depend on them to create the survey and evaluation tools, share the analysis process, and thank them when they bring you information. If they are unable to keep up with your evaluation needs, or you are looking for professional help beginning a program, independent museum professionals provide these services. Many colleges and universities regularly offer very affordable, perhaps free, evaluation services as part of their students' coursework. Choosing the evaluation tools early in your project planning phase will help you allow time and resources to evaluate your work conscientiously.

SOLVING THE CHICKEN-EGG DILEMMA

How can you prove that you can manage a grant before you ever have a grant? You prove you can manage a similar project. Surely you have some to your credit that demonstrate your ability to plan, manage, and complete similar work. If you want a building grant, point out previous successful installations of accessible bathrooms, ramps, and parking spaces; reinstalled galleries; or repaired roofs and replanted landscapes. Each of these undertakings required project design and budgeting, obtaining permits, completing historic commission hearings, hiring contractors, scheduling and overseeing work, and managing expense and cash flow.

If you are after education support, you should have quite a roster of successes in planning and implementing programs. Your annual lecture series requires advance booking for speakers, carefully timed promotional work, and thoughtful planning for accompanying exhibits and gift shop items. Explain how you researched, planned, and installed the visitors' center exhibit on time and within budget. Use examples of "business-as-usual" activities to prove you are worthy of funding for a next-level concept.

SIGNS OF A WORTHY INVESTMENT

Remember, the donor wants results from this investment. Bulletproof planning is a good motivator for funders. That's easy if you can produce the planning documents and explain where your project fits within the plans. Describe how you developed the plans and what components you have already implemented. If years one and two of your strategic plan were focused on developing a volunteer program, community events, and individual giving, describe your success. Explain how those experiences were helpful during your annual review of the plan and led a natural progression into years three and four when you developed an interpretive plan and then used your first major gifts to complete an exhibit or period room reinstallation following that plan. Show how these successes build on each other and create momentum.

The relation between the organizational mission and the plan's goals are as important as the results of the goals. You must create a document that helps you make decisions about allocation of talent and resources when you are faced with choices and opportunities.

If you are missing some plans, like a strategic or interpretive plan, explain how you will develop it. Perhaps you will create a collections policy after you complete an NEH Preservation and Access project. Maybe your staff is taking special training before developing your interpretive plan. What do you do if your board or staff is reluctant to go through an institutional assessment process? Let them hear from others who have been through it and understand its value, as well as its challenges. Visit that organization or invite someone to come speak to your group. Learn what you can about the process and hope that the discussion makes everyone more comfortable with assessment in general and leads you closer to trying it. A grant of technical assistance funds from foundations or the local government can solve two problems—triggering an important process and acquiring your first grant award!

Government programs and special-interest funders are excellent sources of support for surveys, assessments, and evaluation because they are committed to supporting field standards. Check their deadlines, talk to their staff, and then create a sequence for acquiring any plans, standards, or reviews you need to implement best practices. Then include at least one plan as a goal in your current work. Move ahead on these one step at a time since the process is as important as the product.

GETTING A SECOND OPINION

Demonstrating others' financial support and recognition is the surest way to secure more from additional funders—the "join a winner" approach. Third-party recognition includes professional, national, or community awards and comments from appealing local, regional, or national leaders. We have seen how Historic Georgetown, Inc., has used the Steven Hart Award from the Colorado Historical Society to acknowledge and encourage donors. Blithewold has a dramatic story to tell showing support—support that helped convince two major regional foundations to make significant investments in the renewed life of this historic property. Here's an excerpt from their organizational description as included in all grant applications:

In 1999, years of deficit operations forced the lay-offs of nearly all full-time Blithewold staff and greatly reduced the number of public programs. The leaders began to seriously consider a proposal to lease the property to a developer—perhaps restricting or prohibiting public access for the future. Worried supporters formed Save Blithewold, Inc., and in just six weeks raised $650,000 in emergency gifts and pledges to acquire a

99-year lease of the property and provide partial operating support. In 2000, Save Blithewold, Inc., obtained its 501(c)(3) status, and by 2002 had nine full-time, twelve part-time and seasonal staff, 200 volunteers and 1000 members.

This helped convince the Champlin Foundation to make a second gift in 2003, this time to the Capital Campaign. Prince Charitable Trusts made a second gift, this time a three-year commitment to supporting operating expenses and to building the endowment—all were significant gifts for an institution developing momentum.

Requests for advice and invitations for comment or to participate in local, regional, or national projects, discussions, or decision making are all endorsements. When someone from Colonial Williamsburg, the state historical society, or the museum of science calls you for advice, this is third-party recognition. If a senator's office regularly checks with you to confirm or collect historical facts, keep a record and get an endorsement or at least a letter of appreciation you can copy for self-promotion. When *Yankee Magazine* or *Sunset* highlights your site, let your press and tourism offices know, and post color copies of the announcement at local hotels, restaurants, and near your entrance. When someone recognizes your institution for its performance and success, broadcast the message.

How do you get these awards and these comments? You have to participate in the wider circle of the community to get noticed. You and your staff should offer workshops and make presentations at local, regional, and national conferences. When you believe you are competitive for regional or national association awards, you should nominate your organization and its publications or projects; submit names of your staff and volunteers; invite the newspaper for an exhibit review; and be sure your institution is considered for your local *"Best of "* each time. If you don't win, you may still gain feedback from the judges or wider recognition within your peer group.

GETTING THE FIRST GRANT

You have to begin somewhere, so for your first application choose either a discrete project that you won't do until the cash comes in, or take a little help from your friends and collaborate on a project with someone who has attracted funding before.

Perhaps you are ready to buy membership management software or PastPerfect; install two new interpretive signs at the riverbank; or pay for the consultant to assess the recent gift of materials to the archives. Your goal is to fund the project. You also want to begin your "supporter's list," establish a record of experience with funders, and begin your foundation fund-raising career.

Your first target may be a first-come, first-served program like the Museum Assistance Program run by the American Association of Museums and funded by IMLS. There is a pool of money to be distributed, and if you apply before it runs out, with all the required components included, you will get a grant. Funders with a special interest in our field of historical museums and agencies may seem like an easy first target, but in competitive funding programs where the whole field is applying for that money, the competition may be too tough for a first "win."

Your community and local foundations know you better and will be more committed to your success. Your chances may be better because of a smaller pool, closer ties, and your ability to distinguish yourself from the competition. For example, when the local branch of a supermarket chain is making amends for drawing shoppers from the old downtown, maybe it will be in-terested in supporting a local history project on the old district. The state's program supporting technology in small businesses will understand the importance of fund-raising software. Cul-tural councils are making microscopic grants these days, but that $200 is enough to pay for a special lecture, and the proposal process is relatively simple. Those applications, though not very lucrative, are good "firsts" for your fledgling program and they get excellent PR through the state.

If you have resources to offer another organization already successful at earning grants, create an opportunity to meet the staff, compare offerings, and see what you can contribute to a program they will try to fund. You may have a great meeting room, more open space, or an audience connection that will help them widen their reach or offer a program more easily. Instead of proposal writing, your staff will contribute time for site manage-ment, mass mailings, or evaluation work. You may be able to add a layer of content that reinvigorates your colleagues' existing pro-gram and can therefore attract new funders. Yes, collaboration is far more complicated than that, but to be competitive you have to create your opportunities.

WHAT IF THE FOUNDATION SAYS NO?

"No" is part of the grant landscape. Get used to it; we all do. When the answer is no, use this as a learning opportunity. Ask questions. Some foundations have a policy against spending the time to respond—perhaps they have too many applicants. Many, though, are helpful and can either speak with you then or set a time for you to phone again. Like an office visit, keep it short, but hang on their every word. You'll collect ideas for applying again for this or another project, and learn how to improve your proposals and your institution or program in their eyes. Use your knowledge of your institution to gauge which parts of their advice are appropriate.

CONCLUSION

This is a long "to-do" list. One person cannot do it all, so be sure to involve board and front-line volunteers, use advisory groups to your advantage, and work with internship programs to address specific needs. Any time you complete one of these tasks, it's to your advantage. And as you complete each of these steps you gain momentum.

Case: Gaining Traction: The Carlisle Historical Society

The Carlisle Historical Society

The Carlisle Historical Society found itself in an awkward position. The town library was relocating during renovations, and the society, with its collections on the library's third floor, would have to move. It would not be invited back, either. Worse, not only did the society need to find a new home, it had to take the library's historical collection *with* it.

With this double whammy, the community developed feelings for the society that had previously gone unnoticed (both the society and the feelings). After a few months of commercial storage, a community member helped barter an opportunity to purchase a multi-period house and barn, on a main road, with some parking, and at a rock-bottom price. With a three-year-old bequest from a longtime resident and the builder's willingness to

The Carlisle Historical Society. Over the centuries the Captain Samuel Heald Homestead (1740, 1788, and 1849), its uses, and its configuration have evolved along with the town. Today it is home to the Carlisle Historical Society, Carlisle, Massachusetts. Courtesy of the Carlisle Historical Society.

forgo a teardown to build a mini-mansion, the society had a home.

Still there was much to do and no staff to do it. The dual need to unpack the collections and assess and inventory them made the society a perfect mission match for collections-care funders on the local and state levels. The local cultural council, the state archives' Documenting Heritage program funded by the National Historical Publications and Records Commission, and a collaborative program between the Bay State Historical League and the Massachusetts Foundation for the Humanities all awarded grants for collections projects within the first twelve months.

Though the institution itself would not yet attract general operating support, its well-designed programs attracted grants. The programs achieved multiple goals by combining

- professional collections surveys and volunteer training
- professional archival training among collaborating agencies in town
- research with public access components such as print and electronic finding aids, an exhibit, and public lectures for professional colleagues and local citizens

Each project satisfied funders' investment needs to improve public access to local history, to provide a charitable edge serving the society's and the town's collections while providing public programs, and to build the society's circle of professional partners and volunteers for future support. Of course, all the projects fulfilled the society's strategic goals of caring for the collection and serving the town.

Suddenly an institution with a budget of less than $20,000 a year, a small volunteer corps of eight, and no staff had three successful grant-funded projects in its repertoire. It had created enough momentum to move from a sleepy third-floor club to a contributor to community life. The townspeople had a phone number to call for information and a hope of getting an answer. Neighbors started to volunteer. Finding board members became easier. The Girl Scouts wanted a badge project. A Boy Scout made a donation box. When the society conducted its first annual appeal eighteen months later, the 180 members contributed $4,200 to general support—not bad for a "new" organization.

For the coming year, the board made plans for a local barn tour in conjunction with its barn-painting appeal. Building on the barn theme, a popular local artist donated a watercolor of the site featuring the historic barn. The gift of its attendant copyrights meant the society could now print and sell cards, calendars, and tote bags on the theme. The graveyard tour was a sellout, and visitors asked for a repeat. Two new Girl Scout groups came. The society's historian organized a New England history book group to meet at the house as a way to offer a program longer than the previous single-day events, and to encourage sustained relationships between the participants and the society. The second year's appeal raised $7,335. Now the challenge became maintaining momentum.

EIGHT

Maintaining Momentum

When the IMLS Conservation Project Support Grant comes in *and* you receive a donation of original furnishings for the main bedroom *and* the local theater company offers to stage a benefit performance on your lawn, you are gaining momentum. When a foundation makes a three-year commitment to fund a staff member, *and* the construction project finishes on time and within budget, *and* your house tour fund-raiser has the largest attendance ever, you are gaining momentum. Now you need to maintain it.

Fair enough—you can sit in the garden with the staff for a celebratory moment after the big bash. Tell each other the positive parting comments from your patrons. Take the next morning to catch up on the details left aside during the run-up to the exhibit or event, but at lunch sit together again to review the experience *and* the progress of the next coup—an upcoming publication, the MAP IV assessment, or the nascent collaboration with the Boys and Girls Clubs.

To maintain momentum, you have to monitor your work, sustain best practices, refresh yourself through innovation and social and professional relevance, brag a little bit, and manage these relationships.

KEEP MONITORING YOUR WORK

Discipline yourself to keep the numbers: attendance, market data, budget details, and evaluation reports. You won't evaluate every installment of every program, but you should create a plan to evaluate all new programs and sections of older programs once yearly, and leave leeway to evaluate areas of curiosity or concern. In Minnesota, the Scott County Historical Society's member survey about museum programming convinced them of the need to provide adult programs in the daytime *and* in the evening hours. Director John Gutterer found that the same program offered at different times reaches very different adult audiences. This reinvigorates programming and can provide encouragement for staff wondering what difference it would make if they didn't decorate for Christmas just this once.

SUSTAIN BEST PRACTICES

When you've done all the surveys and assessments and established all the policies, what's left? Maintaining standards. Review your institutional plans; keep your advisory boards active; keep operating procedures up-to-date by reviewing the ethics statement with new staff and volunteers and reminding longer-term staff that these policies exist; practice emergency procedures and include the training in your annual training schedule;

and keep looking for new twists on the old themes. You may have finished the MAP assessments years ago but wish for a little re-tuning. Why not invite an expert to review part of your organiza-tion's work, just as a refresher? This could be an even exchange of talent or a collegial contribution from one professional to an-other. Attend conferences and meetings yourself or send the staff. The problem with standards is that they keep changing. You and your staff need to be aware of those changes to be able to adapt appropriately.

You cannot avoid the stark but simple truth that to maintain momentum, you must do everything well. For Nina Zannieri at the Paul Revere Memorial Association (PRMA), that means "every-thing . . . from a well-conceived grant request to a lecture, and from public programs to research. It is doing what you can do well rather than trying to do everything." She is careful to listen to staff "when they say 'enough'" and in return has staff that "work plenty of extra hours" but under their own motivation to do an excellent job on "projects that they [and the organization] believe in." Of course, the definition of quality changes too, so monitoring leadership work at your colleagues' institutions will keep complacency at bay.

REFRESH YOUR WORK

Refresh yourself and your organization through innovation and through social and professional relevance. Management consul-tant Laura Roberts encourages boards to spend fifteen minutes of every meeting talking about what else is going on in the com-munity. This exercise in thinking about your environment, your relationships with other groups, and their relative successes and failures is important. It leads to new ideas in collaboration, programming, and funding; averts costly competition, and combats the self-centeredness and inward thinking that can besiege any of our organizations. You and your board members should seek opportunities to help out on award panels, as peer reviewers for grants, and as judges for other honors.

Innovate from a position of strength, not desperation. Zannieri believes part of maintaining momentum is finding new ways to do what you are already good at. In her case, that involves creative collaborative ventures with the Institute of Contemporary Art and Boston Landmarks Orchestra—"all very mission related." These provide expanded visibility, new audiences, *and* introduce PRMA to new funders.

Can you try a radically new program? For decades, house museums interpreted the owners' lives and ignored the lives of the "help." Now, tours of staff quarters have earned equal time and often prove the most popular. Hopefully your mission gives you the opportunity to innovate. In 1986 the PRMA added neighborhood context to its mission statement, making it manageable in scope yet broad enough to try new programming.

> The purpose of the Association is the pursuit of historical interests with particular attention to the life and work of Paul Revere and his family, the nature of life in early Boston, and the history of Boston's North End Community; the preservation of the Paul Revere House and the Hichborn House as historical and architectural landmarks; and the education of the public through the presentation of programs, exhibitions, publications and collections.

As a mature institution, it had the experience and resources to exploit these new possibilities without being overwhelmed by them.

Paul Revere House, Paul Revere Memorial Association, Boston, Massachusetts. The house was built around 1680 for Boston merchant Robert Howard. When Paul Revere purchased the property in 1770, it had undergone several changes. He owned the building until 1800. During that time Revere excelled in the art of silversmithing while participating actively in the rebellion and the Revolution. The House is a National Historic Landmark. Courtesy of the Paul Revere Memorial Association.

BRAG

You should have a strong media contact list and excellent relationships with each outlet. They should see you as a reliable source. In turn, the coverage is fair and informed when you make the news. Are you known as an excellent resource for images and quotes each time the anniversary of the flood rolls around? Do the preservationists count on you for a poignant early photo of the doomed house at the corner? When the paper is preparing its list of vacation activities for kids, does the columnist already have your information and a great photo in hand? As for news copy, when you pull off a state appropriation, preempt the journalist's stance against entitlement by providing the whole story on your need and value. In your suggestions for topical articles on upcoming projects, be sure to brag by paying thanks to your funders.

In your own materials, draw attention to staff achievements when you're announcing your institution's accomplishments. Enter your exhibits, programs, and printed and Web materials in competitions that reach a wider audience. When you win a federal grant, be sure the representative or senator who wrote the supporting letter gets a thank you from you and a board member. That way he or she knows you appreciate the help *and* knows you won a grant—something he or she will share with constituents.

MANAGE RELATIONSHIPS

That sort of information sharing is relationship management. As your success grows, so will the list of relationships to nurture. Now you have to manage the existing relationships even as you develop new ones. The commitment in time and energy is phenomenal; it easily becomes the executive director's major preoccupation. The whole of your institution should feel responsible for contributing to fund-raising.

Let your staff and volunteers share appropriate responsibility. Everyone is responsible for making or sharing contacts. They should notice on the radio, in printed materials, and in peer-group meetings where others raise their money—special events, sponsorships, and foundations. Board members must regularly and continually help identify and cultivate connections either in response to your research or through their own circulation in the community. They should participate in meetings with funders, and provide letters of introduction, support, and thanks as necessary. Staff will research potential donors, keep the information updated and manageable, oversee meeting arrangements, and prepare and send materials. Sometimes they will write the proposals; sometimes the director does; but no one person raises money alone.

CONCLUSION

Maintaining momentum may *seem* easier than creating it, but it isn't. Funders and everyone else keep moving the goal posts. It happens in every other profession as well. Reaching the top of your game and staying there requires continuous hard, good work. Fortunately, there are moments when the check comes in and you feel renewed and reinvigorated, not to mention vindicated.

Best wishes for *your* good work.

Appendix A:
Proposal Preparation Tips

With the variety of funders' expectations, each proposal will be individualized. Still, some basic concepts apply generally to proposal writing.

THE BASICS

The Laws of Proposal Writing

- Call the funder to discuss your application. Apply only if you receive positive feedback. In this competitive market, hesitation is not encouragement. Though there are other reasons than money for making grant applications, a cash grant is your primary goal and only likely if your contact is very positive about your planned proposal.
- Check the deadline. Does it mean receipt date or postmark?

- Skim the application guidelines and forms. Make a list of both the required and appropriate attachments and begin to collect or create them early. For example, as soon as possible, ask your senator or a colleague for a letter of support if appropriate, convert your color prints to color slides and black and white photos, and get your hands on the required official documents such as National Register certification. Give your colleagues as much warning as possible if you need their help collecting these materials.

- Prepare the budget. This helps you organize your project and refine the request amount. Remember that a complete budget shows both expenses and income, cash, and in-kind contributions. Be sure you know what the funder considers eligible costs.

- Now reread the guidelines and highlight key concepts and distinctive language for making your case.

- Find out who reviews the proposals, if you can. Do they have any knowledge of your field? Your best bet is to write to an intelligent reader but not assuming she or he knows your site or understands your field particularly well. Write concisely and without jargon.

- If it is a peer review program, speak with the program staff to determine the criteria for reviewer selection and to learn about review tendencies common to this program. You may discover that peer review panels regularly complain about the lack of innovative applications or the abundance of Web-based projects.

- Begin writing when, and only when, you can say in one sentence what you plan to do, as well as where, why, when, how, and for whom you will do it.

- Leave no questions unanswered for your reader.

- Write the summary statement last.

- Ask a colleague (preferably one not intimate with the project) to read a draft in order to point out confusing parts, unanswered questions, and redundancies.
- Proofread in print; never proof on-screen. Better yet, have someone unfamiliar with the proposal do the proofing.
- Give your project a decent, memorable, short, descriptive name to help the funder identify you among the hordes.
- Submit proposals on time, if not early. Triple check to be sure you've included all the components. Use the recommended delivery method. Submit the required number of copies. Use paperclips, not staples, so the recipient can separate the proposal pages to copy them as needed. Any bindings are sure to be thrown away, so waste no effort on them. Send videos or audio support materials *only* if requested by the funder. If you want something returned, include a self-addressed envelope with the appropriate amount of postage.

WRITING

When They Want a Letter of Inquiry First

A letter of inquiry is a formal request to apply. You must convince the funder that the proposed project fits within the mission, scope, and interests of the funder, that you have a well-thought-out project and the resources to succeed with it, and that reading and considering a more involved proposal is worth their staff time.

Keep the letter to two pages. Start with your elevator speech, back it up with evidence of need and of your ability, explain what would happen if you do not proceed with the project, and ask if you may submit a proposal. Be sure you remember to include specifics like your organization's description and nonprofit status; the project's date, location, and audience; outcomes; and the total budget and the amount you would like to request. Do not send any unrequested materials.

That's a great deal of information to put cleanly and coherently in two pages, but it's an excellent exercise in honing your descriptions of your organization and your project. If you can't describe your work in a readable letter, your proposal will be difficult to follow *or* fund. Keep the original long drafts of this to use when preparing the complete proposals—if you are invited to apply.

Completing a Provided Proposal Form

If the funder provides a form, use it. Diverging from it can be reason to disqualify you. If the funder suggests a common proposal format, it is reasonable to use it. Uniformity helps the funder compare proposals and make decisions comfortably. Depend upon your program's value and the style and quality of your writing to distinguish your organization.

Writing a Free-form Proposal

If the funder does not provide an application form, make the whole proposal either a three-page letter or a single-page cover letter with three or more proposal pages following. Any additional information can be appended as lists, descriptions of exhibits, or statistics about the proposed project. If the guidelines suggest "topics to be addressed" or "evaluation criteria," use those as headings for organizing your draft's outline. Depending upon the funder's wording and your writing style, you may edit these into softer headings or leave them in as bold section breaks in the narrative. Save this early outline of the proposal so that when someone suggests removing a necessary section, you know why not to.

Organizing Your Proposal

I use this sequence most often:

1. Cover Letter
2. Proposal with
   A. Summary statement
   B. Introduction to my institution and the situation
   C. Problem statement and chosen solution
   D. Explain the steps we'll take and the difference that will make
   E. Budget and future funding
   F. Describe evaluation process and expectations
   G. Remind them of the request
   H. Conclusion
3. Attachments (if this is long, then I include an attachment list in the proposal cover letter or as a cover to this section)
4. Their required pieces
5. A compelling image or support letter as appropriate
6. Any appendixes

Start with a short cover letter introducing yourself, reminding the reader of any past connections you share, and explaining very briefly what the attached proposal will request. Remember, though, this finely crafted letter may not get copied for all the readers to see, so you'll be making that pitch again at the beginning of your proposal. These busy people need to understand the proposal immediately or they may struggle to appreciate it. Struggling inhibits check writing.

Organize your proposal in a sequence that makes the most sense for describing your project, but do use sensible chronology. A lost reader can at least hold onto the sequence of your site's origins, your organizational history, and your current challenges until they can visualize and understand your message.

Start with that summary paragraph telling the reader *who* is asking for *how* much money and in *what* way it will solve which problems (the *why*), plus *where* and *when* you will do all this. That is your elevator pitch, your thirty seconds to instill your message. Here's an example of the elevator pitch:

> In honor of the 60th D-Day celebrations, the Herne Bay Historical Society's "WWII from Home" project will train fifteen adult and teen community volunteers in collecting oral histories from Herne Bay residents who were children during WWII. The Society would like to apply to the Mayor's Fund for $5,000 for oral history training, purchase of five Sony Walkman recorders, and printing 3,000 copies of a book of reminiscences. The project takes place from January to June 2003 with publication in January 2004. Income from the book sales will fund future oral history collecting and publication projects.

Introduce Yourself

Provide background information on your site and your organization as it applies to the current situation and the proposal. If you really feel a need to provide more information, it may be more appropriate in an institutional fact sheet you attach as an appendix. Those readers who need that information will look for it there; those who don't will be happy without it.

Identify the Problem and Describe Your Solution

Familiarize the reader with the need you will address or the problem you will solve. Use information from your external research on the field, trends, and society to make your case. In addition to the great anecdotes you've collected, use supporting material that demonstrates that a funder doesn't have to take your word for it. Identify others who have recognized the problem and called for a solution.

It's easy to be so focused on explaining what you will do that you forget to show *how* what you do will make a difference for whomever you serve (or in your ability to serve) and why that change is good. Yes, the project will make a difference for your institution, but it must be a difference that increases your ability to fulfill your mission. Explain what the project does for your audience, not just for the institution.

Explain how you are unique, but only if it's true. If you don't know how or whether you are unique, do some serious research, document it well, and then use it. If you are not unique, talk about the similarities and differences between your program and others'. Tell the reader about the good strong leaders that make your organization best suited to do this important job.

Convert the reader. Statistics, stories, comparisons, and images help you make your case. Every reader learns in a different way or is convinced in a different way. Use stories *and* numbers to make your argument so that you score with both types of learners. Convince them by leaving no room for doubt, and answer all their questions before any come into their minds. You can use those questions as section headings, if you like. For example, "Why is the Sandwich Glass Museum best suited for this project?" Or: "Isn't anyone else doing this?" Then answer the question.

Methods and the Difference

This section describes what you're going to do, and why the selected activities and sequencing are appropriate. It includes description of who does what when, either in narrative form or a timeline. The guidelines may or may not require a time chart. If they do not, but your list is complicated or lengthy, add one yourself.

Boldly point out what difference your program makes as a lead in to the next section on evaluating your success. You should describe goals and objectives here.

Evaluation

This field is evolving rapidly, so make it an important part of your work to keep abreast of changes. Evaluation is one way the funder can quantify return on investment. If your project is an exhibit or a major new program, be sure to include front-end, formative, and summative evaluation (see chapter 4). Wherever possible, employ outcome-based evaluation for measuring the degree of impact, learning, or change your programs have on your participants. The funder may provide criteria or let you establish desirable outcome values yourself. If your project is construction, then the work schedule is your evaluation tool. Be able to explain that you met the schedule and budget, or be able to explain what reasonably changed your schedule.

Budget and Future Funding

Again, a budget has income and outgo. Remember to include the request amounts you're submitting to other funders to make up the balance with notification dates included. Value in-kind contributions at what it would cost you to purchase those same goods or services. If someone gives you the clapboards at cost, then include the cost as a cash expense, and the discount as an in-kind contribution.

Explain your budget so that if one part is extraordinarily expensive, or not, the reader understands your pricing and believes you. If the funder provides a budget form with too little room to break out important costs, you can do the breakout in the narrative. For example, "materials" on a greenhouse construction budget can be varied and substantial. Pointing out the costs for cyprus, glass engineered to code, and the special type of brick will help the reader understand why that line item is so large.

If you are applying for support for a project continuing beyond the life of this grant, be sure to let the funder know how you plan to continue funding it. Part of your answer will be "we will continue to look for funding to support our educational programs." The other part will be an explanation that costs will be less in the second year since there is far less development time required, or what other funders you will approach next year, or if an education endowment will begin supporting projects like these in two years. You need a plan to fund it; why not develop it now and reassure your potential funder?

Remember to Ask Again

Repeat your request near the conclusion, using somewhat different language. Explain where else you are looking for, or have found, money. The tightrope between what you need and what you can get is never easy to negotiate. If you cannot possibly get from this funder all that you need, make sure the reader knows where you are looking for the rest of it. During your phone call, test your request amount on your foundation contact for an indication of its appropriateness. Hopefully you have enough good funder targets to fully fund, perhaps overfund, the project. The funders understand this.

If you fully fund the project before that last donor reviews your application, call your contact at the foundation. Let them know what has happened and then discuss how to proceed. If you actually overfund a project, the last check received is the overbalance. Contact the donor to discuss the degree of over-funding, the possible options for reserving or using the funds, and the donor's preference on how to proceed. Funders will appreciate your honesty and your care for its institutional resources, and will either help you redirect the proposal or will look on you fondly for the next application.

Your Conclusion

Don't wince here. Be sure to include a "thank you for considering this proposal" or "thank you for your time" and a sincere "happy to show you the museum" or "would be pleased to visit you at your convenience." Provide a direct-line phone number. An honest flourish is appropriate: "If Sandwich Glass Museum doesn't offer these programs, who else can?"

What if You're Applying for Continued Support of the Same Project?

A lot of materials have passed through the funder's office since you last applied, so treat a second application on a project as new to the readers. If you have a chance, talk to the funder to find out what the organization likes about the program, and even ask what they would like to see in your next proposal.

If there are changes to the program, explain why you are making the changes as you explain what they are and what difference they make. If there will be nothing new to the program, be sure in this subsequent proposal to update all other information:

- Check the budget and attendance numbers, participants' names, locations, anything that may have changed since the last proposal.
- Use participants' comments as second opinions of your programs' value.
- Include quotes about new studies and statistics showing the continuing or growing need for the program in your community.
- Point out how the original concepts remain important, perhaps more so because you discovered the program worked better than you had expected or because it produced additional and useful good results (otherwise known as positive outcomes).

When writing about a project for the umpteenth time, use a proposal checklist to uncover missing sections you might have deleted because they've come to bore you. Those details may seen superfluous to you but *not* to the reader. The Grantsmanship Center's Proposal Checklist is an excellent tool for identifying missing sections.

WRITING STYLE AND TRICKS

Read widely to get into your subject and to take you in new directions with your programs and grants. Identify other organizations that have won grants for related projects. Collect current opinion and research from the field relating to your area of work.

Prepare your workplace and work time. Take at least two hours together for writing, but no more than three or four or you may burn out. Write alone, in a room with a "do not disturb" sign on the door, e-mail off, and the phone blocked. Music helps some writers. If there is no door to your office, good headphones and the right music can make all the difference.

Once Again, with Feeling: Start with the Budget!

Budget development helps you to:

- include all the necessary parts of a project
- realize what hasn't been thought out yet
- compare what parts might be out of proportion
- decide what each donor's financial part will be

Writing

Begin when you can successfully describe a real need, by a clearly definable audience, that you can easily address, with a sensible budget in support of your mission and your donor's. When you can answer that question using only one sentence, you can get started. If not, keep refining it before you try to sell it. This research and refinement is a warm-up to writing so that when you begin, the computer screen is not blank too long.

After the budget and the single-sentence description, you can start writing wherever you want. It may be the middle, the evaluation section, or the ending flourish. Just get started.

If you have a great idea but just can't find the right place for it, cut and paste it to the end of the application in case you find the right spot later. Forcing it to fit early on will only interrupt your writing flow.

When you are having trouble paring down the proposal, perhaps the words you are most proud of are the problem. They may be too heavy or complicated. Cut and paste those down to the bottom of the document, too. You will not lose them, but you can try to live without them. You may find a way to keep the idea with fewer words.

Remember, writing is a skill that you develop over time and polish with use. It gets easier the more you do it. Good luck!

Appendix B:
Resources

This is a personal list of my favorite, most often accessed resources for information and updates. The list includes online publications, organizations, and books. The links may change, but are correct at the moment of writing.

ONLINE PUBLICATIONS

"Inspiring Learning for All" by the Museums, Libraries and Archives Council (U.K.), www.inspiringlearningforall.gov.uk
"The Kellogg Foundation's Evaluation Handbook," www.wkkf .org/Publications/evalhdbk/default.htm

ORGANIZATIONAL OR INFORMATIONAL SITES

www.aam-us.org   American Association of Museums

www.aaslh.org	American Association for State and Local History
www.cof.org	The Council on Foundations is a membership group for grant-making organizations. It's a great source of advice on the details of foundations and on the world they operate in. It has a community foundation finder page
www.ed.gov	U.S. Department of Education
www.fedgrants.gov	A resource for federal funding opportunities with a searchable database for grant notices plus the subscription point for an applicant notifier e-mail list
http://factfinder.census.gov	U.S. Census online; for describing your target audience using demographics
www.fdncenter.org	The Foundation Center: An excellent resource for organizations and individuals looking for grant support and for funders. Timely information on philanthropy and the nonprofit sector. They offer proposal writing and development workshops, and have a substantial publications list and excellent on-line resources, including an excellent subscription database of foundation funders
www.grantcraft.org	The Ford Foundation's website to help grant makers and applicants.

It has great information that grant seekers should read to help them understand grant makers and what they are looking for in fundable organizations

www.grants.gov — This federal government website is a searchable source for grant deadlines and descriptions for the federal grant-making agencies

www.grantsalert.com — Website and e-mail update on federal grant deadlines

www.tgci.org — The Grantsmanship Center, Inc.: workshops and publications on proposal writing for government and foundation sources

www.guidestar.org — Guidestar: a national database of nonprofit organizations for grant makers, individual donors, and nonprofits with a subscription-based searchable foundation database, useful articles and tips

www.imls.gov — Institute of Museum and Library Services: description of grant programs and deadlines, list of awardees, sample grants, evaluation tools and a planning tutorial

www.arts.gov — National Endowment for the Arts

www.neh.gov — National Endowment for the Humanities

www.not-for-profit.org — The Nonprofit Resource Center: This is a one-stop directory for

Internet resources for nonprofit
organizations

www.unitedway.org   The United Way: for outcomes
measurement ideas

BOOKS

Barbato, Joseph, and Danielle S. Furlich. *Writing for a Good Cause:
The Complete Guide to Crafting Proposals and Other Persuasive
Pieces for Non-Profits* (New York: Simon and Schuster, 2000).

Borun, Minda, and Randi Korn, eds. *Introduction to Museum Evaluation.* Committee on Audience Research and Evaluation Professional Practice Series, ed. Roxana Adams (Washington, D.C.:
American Association of Museums, 1999).

Brown, Larissa Golden, and Martin John Brown. *Demystifying Grant
Seeking: What You REALLY Need to Do to Get Grants* (San Francisco: Jossey-Bass, 2001).

Collins, Sarah, ed. *The Foundation Center's Guide to Winning Proposals* (New York: Foundation Center, 2003).

Program Planning & Proposal Writing, Expanded Version (Los Angeles: Grantsmanship Center, 2004).

Proposal Checklist & Evaluation Form (Los Angeles: Grantsmanship
Center, 1988).

Simon, Judith Sharken, with J. Terence Donovan. *The Five Life Stages
of Nonprofit Organizations: Where You Are, Where You're Going,
and What to Expect When You Get There* (St. Paul, Minn.: Amherst
H. Wilder Foundation, 2001).

Index

501(c)(3) status, 50, 108, 131

AAM. *See* American Association of Museums
AAMD. *See* Association of Art Museum Directors
AASLH. *See* American Association for State and Local History
accreditation, 6, 44, 98–99
advisory boards, 25, 59, 92
agenda for donor meetings, 27–28
Alswang, Hope, 104n3
American Association for State and Local History (AASLH), 61, 66–71, 73, 99, 114, 180

Association of Art Museum Directors (AAMD), 90
American Association of Museums (AAM), 50, 90, 98–99, 150, 179
Anderson, Judy, 22
annual appeal, 14
Arts Council England, 62
Association of Science-Technology Centers (ASTC), 90
ASTC. *See* Association of Science-Technology Centers
attachments to proposals, 166
audience, 5, 6, 52, 56–59, 142
awards, 114–115, 148–150

Baldwin, Cinda, 135
Bay State Historical League, 154
Bell County Historical Society,
73, 128
best practices, 158
Blithewold Mansion, Gardens &
Arboretum, 72–73, 80–81,
102, 107–11, 148
board, 45, 80, 90–92, 95, 163;
assessing grant-readiness,
43–44
Bombardieri, Marcella, 21
The Boston Globe, 21–22
brag, 162
budget, 121–22, 166, 169,
172–73, 175, 176; multi-
year, 96; operating, 88, 89,
94
budgeting for grants, 49
"Building an Organization to
Last: Reflections & Lessons
Learned From SeaChange,"
80, 92

calling foundations, 29–30, 165,
173
Carlisle Historical Society, 83,
93, 139, 153–55
Census, U. S., 144, 180
Center for Effective
Philanthropy, 81
Champlin Foundations, 149
Chen-Courtin, Dorothy, 22, 60,
122

collaborate, 26, 102, 151, 157,
160
Colorado Historical Society, 72,
114, 148
common proposal format, 168
community foundation, 9, 13
compliance, 49–50
Connecticut Humanities
Council, 96
Conner Prairie, 18, 35, 54–58,
61, 64–65, 73, 82, 128–29,
135–38
consultants, 92
contingency fees, 128
contract, grant as a, 51
Corning Museum of Glass, 77
costs, eligible, 166
Council on Foundations, 180
Courson, Bruce, 75–77
cultivation, 3, 11, 21, 26–27, 48,
163
curriculum frameworks, 54

deadlines, 165, 166
Department of Education, 144,
180
dependability, 87–90
Direct Marketing Association,
142
documentation, 62, 140–45
donor interests, 15

earned income, 14, 96, 104
earned revenue, 89

About the Author

Sarah S. Brophy is a long-time freelance proposal writer for New England museums, tribes, municipalities, and cultural resource organizations. She holds a master of arts in American History from the College of William & Mary, Virginia, and a Certificate in History Administration from the Colonial Williamsburg Foundation. When she was a museum employee, she worked at historical institutions in Massachusetts, Colorado, New York, and Virginia.

Her most favorite grant application won $440,000 from the National Endowment for the Humanities.